WebAssembly Essentials

Make code reusable and deployed for high performance web apps

AF527179

Emrys Callahan

GitforGits™
ASIAN PUBLISHING HOUSE

Published by: GitforGits
Publisher: Sonal Dhandre
www.gitforgits.com
support@gitforgits.com

Printed in India

First Printing: October 2023

ISBN: 978-8119177257

Cover Design by: Kitten Publishing

Prologue

In the ever-evolving landscape of software development, staying abreast of the latest tools and techniques is paramount. This is the age where the distinctions between web and native applications are beginning to blur. As developers, the tools at our disposal can make or break our creations. Welcome to "WebAssembly Essentials," the definitive guide for modern developer's eager to explore the revolutionary world of WebAssembly (Wasm) and its vast potential.

Historically, the web has been dominated by JavaScript, a language that's both loved and loathed in equal measure. As versatile as JavaScript is, it comes with limitations, especially when it comes to performance-intensive applications. Enter WebAssembly - a beacon of hope for those yearning for near-native performance on the web. The idea is tantalizing: take code from languages like C++, Rust, or even Python, and run it in the browser at blistering speeds. It sounds ambitious, and indeed, the journey to make this a reality was filled with challenges and innovations. But the fruits of these endeavors are nothing short of spectacular.

This book unfolds as a meticulously curated detailed walkthrough, designed to cater to both newcomers and seasoned developers. It presents a blend of fundamental concepts, practical illustrations, and advanced strategies. Embark on a journey that commences with the very essence of WebAssembly, gradually leading you into deeper waters, where you'll learn to navigate the complexities with confidence and expertise. A significant portion of our exploration focuses on tools and their mastery. You will delve into the intricate workings of tools like Emscripten and Binaryen, which act as powerful bridges, facilitating the transformation of code from various languages into Wasm. But tools are just the beginning. The real magic lies in understanding the myriad techniques to port applications into the Wasm format, unlocking an entirely new realm of web application potential. Whether it's a C++ game, a Python machine learning model, or a Java-based enterprise application, the promise of bringing them to the web with near-native performance is now a tangible reality.

But what about JavaScript? Fear not, for the story of WebAssembly isn't one of replacement but of collaboration. We venture into the world of Wasm bindings, illustrating how JavaScript and WebAssembly can coexist and collaborate, ensuring smooth communication between modules and enhancing the versatility of your applications.

Performance optimization, a topic that resonates with every developer, receives special attention. From strategies for fine-tuning your code to techniques like multi-threading that allow for parallel operations, we ensure that your applications don't just run—they soar. We also touch upon concepts like lazy loading and code splitting, ensuring optimal responsiveness and efficient load times, culminating in a sublime user experience. Diving deeper, we explore the nuances of memory management in Wasm, providing insights into efficient utilization of resources. This is complemented by a comprehensive detailed walkthrough on leveraging browser developer tools, empowering you to dissect, analyze, and further enhance the performance of your applications.

Finally, we address an aspect vital to modern web applications: caching. In an age of instant gratification, ensuring rapid and efficient access to web applications is essential. Through effective caching strategies tailored for Wasm, we guide you in enhancing accessibility and user experience. "WebAssembly Essentials" is more than just a book; it's a journey—a journey that promises to equip you with the knowledge, tools, and best practices to redefine what's possible on the web. So, we shall embark on this adventure together, delving into the world of WebAssembly, where the future of web development beckons.

Content

Preface

Dive deep into the fundamentals as you explore the core concepts of WebAssembly and its role in the modern web landscape. Witness firsthand the potential of this bytecode, designed to execute at near-native speed, and understand its pivotal role in bridging the gap between web and native applications.

Chapter-wise, you will be treated to a systematic breakdown of tools and techniques. Beginning with introductions to foundational tools like Emscripten and Binaryen, the book offers hands-on approaches to compile applications from various languages to Wasm. Delve further to unearth nuances of bindings, helping your JavaScript and WebAssembly modules communicate seamlessly. As you progress, unearth strategies to optimize your code, explore multi-threading and parallelism, and leverage modern web techniques like lazy loading and code splitting, all within the context of WebAssembly. Memory management, a challenge in many programming paradigms, is addressed with finesse, offering you conceptual and practical insights.

To ensure your WebAssembly applications are performing at their peak, the book dedicates chapters to profiling, benchmarking, and browser tool integration. Learn to dissect performance bottlenecks and finetune every byte of your application. You will be armed with best practices, common pitfalls, and solutions to ensure the journey from native code to browser execution is smooth and efficient.

In this book you will learn:

- WebAssembly Fundamentals: Grasp Wasm's core concepts, bridging web and native apps, boosting performance seamlessly.
- Tool Mastery: Dive into tools like Emscripten and Binaryen, facilitating efficient cross-language compilations to Wasm.
- Language Porting: Learn techniques to convert C++, Python, and Java apps, unlocking web application potential.
- Wasm Bindings: Seamlessly integrate JavaScript and WebAssembly, ensuring smooth inter-module communications.
- Optimization Techniques: Harness strategies for fine-tuning code, guaranteeing peak application performance.
- Parallelism and Threading: Explore multi-threading, leveraging simultaneous operations, accelerating execution times.
- Advanced Loading: Implement lazy loading and code splitting, optimizing web app responsiveness and load times.
- Memory Management: Dive deep into efficient memory usage, ensuring resourceful application execution.

- ❖ Performance Analysis: Proficiently use browser developer tools, dissecting and enhancing application performance.
- ❖ Caching Strategies: Enhance user experience with effective caching, ensuring rapid web application accessibility.

In essence, "WebAssembly Essentials" is a must-have companion for anyone aiming to elevate their web applications. Get ready to embark on a transformative journey, turning your existing projects into browser-compatible powerhouses with ease and precision.

GitforGits

Prerequisites

This book is for every programmer aspiring to put their all applications onto web browser with the same speed, efficiency and product performance. Knowing fundamentals of any programming language and basics of web app development is sufficient to tear out the book wholly.

Codes Usage

Are you in need of some helpful code examples to assist you in your programming and documentation? Look no further! Our book offers a wealth of supplemental material, including code examples and exercises.

Not only is this book here to aid you in getting your job done, but you have our permission to use the example code in your programs and documentation. However, please note that if you are reproducing a significant portion of the code, we do require you to contact us for permission.

But don't worry, using several chunks of code from this book in your program or answering a question by citing our book and quoting example code does not require permission. But if you do choose to give credit, an attribution typically includes the title, author, publisher, and ISBN. For example, "WebAssembly Essentials by Emrys Callahan".

If you are unsure whether your intended use of the code examples falls under fair use or the permissions outlined above, please do not hesitate to reach out to us at support@gitforgits.com.

We are happy to assist and clarify any concerns.

Acknowledgement

I owe a tremendous debt of gratitude to GitforGits, for their unflagging enthusiasm and wise counsel throughout the entire process of writing this book. Their knowledge and careful editing helped make sure the piece was useful for people of all reading levels and comprehension skills. In addition, I'd like to thank everyone involved in the publishing process for their efforts in making this book a reality. Their efforts, from copyediting to advertising, made the project what it is today.

Finally, I'd like to express my gratitude to everyone who has shown me unconditional love and encouragement throughout my life. Their support was crucial to the completion of this book. I appreciate your help with this endeavour and your continued interest in my career.

Chapter 1: Introduction to WebAssembly

Web Development before WebAssembly

The World Wide Web has developed into an essential component of all of our lives in this age of information technology. It is essential to take a step back and gain an understanding of the landscape of web development that existed prior to the inception of WebAssembly before delving into the complexities of WebAssembly itself. By doing so, we are able to gain a comprehensive understanding of the revolutionary effect that WebAssembly has had on the development of modern websites.

Static web pages, which were primarily composed of HTML and CSS, were what defined the early stages of the World Wide Web. They focused primarily on imparting knowledge but lacked the interactive features that have become standard fare in modern times. When it was first released in the middle of the 1990s, JavaScript quickly established itself as the go-to tool for web developers seeking to create interactive and dynamic websites. JavaScript was able to expand its capabilities alongside the development of browsers, which in turn made it possible to create web applications with a higher level of complexity.

Rise of JavaScript

Because of the rise of JavaScript, web applications started becoming more complex and packed with a variety of features. JavaScript's capabilities have been further enhanced by tools and frameworks such as jQuery, Angular, and React, which have made it possible for developers to create sophisticated Single Page Applications (SPAs). The internet was no longer used solely for the purpose of consuming content; rather, it evolved into a platform for the deployment of powerful applications, such as graphic editors and real-time collaboration tools. On the other hand, as the complexity of applications increased, the visibility of JavaScript's limitations increased as well. It was clear that there were bottlenecks in performance, particularly in computationally intensive activities. Web developers looked for ways to execute code more quickly and effectively, which led to the creation of JavaScript engines like Google's V8. Despite these improvements, JavaScript was still limited in some ways, primarily because it was not intended from the beginning to handle the intensive computational work that is required of modern web applications.

Around the same time, there was a growing interest in bringing applications to the web that weren't initially written for the web environment. Specifically, this interest was focused on bringing desktop-based applications to the web. These included computer simulations, video games, and applications with a heavy reliance on graphics. The goal of the developers was to take advantage of the vast potential of the web without having to completely rewrite their applications in JavaScript. Tools such as Adobe Flash and Java Applets attempted to fill this gap, but they were plagued with performance and security issues and ultimately failed. The most significant obstacle consisted of getting code to run in the browser at speeds that were close to those of the underlying hardware while still retaining all of its power. Applications written in languages such as C, C++, and Rust would be able to run without any problems in the web environment if this were to take place. In addition, the web required a binary format that, in contrast to the text-based JavaScript, would make it possible to achieve significantly faster load times.

In an effort to improve performance, Mozilla developed ASM.js, a subset of JavaScript that gave developers the ability to write code that would execute at speeds that were nearly identical to those of the native platform. This was an early indication that the web was prepared to move beyond the limitations that JavaScript imposed. Concurrently, Google announced the Portable Native Client, or PNaCl, with the intention of running C and C++ code in the browser in a secure and effective manner. Nevertheless, despite the fact that both of these solutions showed promise, they each had certain limitations and were unable to win over the support of all of the major web browsers.

Vision for Unified Web Standard

The difficulties and experiments that took place over the course of the preceding years crystallized into a need that was crystal clear: the world wide web required a universal, efficient, and safe standard that was capable of bringing nearly native performance to browsers. This wasn't just about improving JavaScript; it was also about rethinking the possibilities of what the web platform as a whole was capable of accomplishing. WebAssembly came into existence as a direct result of the convergence of a number of different people's experiences, needs, and ideas. When viewed against this backdrop, WebAssembly emerged not as a simple replacement for JavaScript but rather as a complementary tool that expanded the possibilities of web development. As we progress through this book, we will learn more about the many facets of WebAssembly, including its architecture, capabilities, and the revolutionary impact it has had on the web as we know it.

Inception and Evolution of WebAssembly

As the digital tapestry of the web grew more intricate, the need for a faster, more efficient computational platform became apparent. Enter WebAssembly: not just an answer to the web's growing pains but a visionary leap forward in what browser-based applications could achieve.

Birth of WebAssembly

The learnings surrounding WebAssembly, often abbreviated as WASM, began in earnest around 2015. This collaborative effort, backed by tech giants like Mozilla, Microsoft, Google, and Apple, was aimed at developing a new binary format for the web. WebAssembly was envisioned as a low-level virtual machine that would run code at near-native speed, opening up the web to languages other than JavaScript. In contrast to ASM.js and PNaCl's earlier attempts to optimize the web's performance, WebAssembly's design was both browser and language-agnostic. This meant that it could run on any browser, allowing developers to write code in multiple languages. By June 2015, the WebAssembly Community Group was formed under W3C, marking a formal step towards realizing this vision.

Design Philosophy behind WebAssembly

WebAssembly was built with several key principles in mind:

- Efficiency and Speed: The primary motivator was to execute code faster than JavaScript, allowing for intensive applications to run smoothly.

- Security: With the drawbacks of tools like Flash in mind, WebAssembly was designed to be secure within the sandboxed environment of a browser.

- Portability and Compactness: It had to work seamlessly across different devices and platforms, with a compact binary format ensuring quicker load times.

- Flexibility: Designed not to replace but to complement JavaScript, WebAssembly aimed to work hand-in-hand with existing web technologies.

By March 2017, WebAssembly had achieved a pivotal moment in its history, attaining the status of an MVP (Minimum Viable Product). This critical milestone meant that the core elements and functionalities were stable and robust enough to be adopted on a broader scale. Notably, support for WebAssembly's MVP was rolled out across all major web browsers—Google Chrome, Mozilla Firefox, Apple Safari, and Microsoft Edge. This widespread acceptance heralded a new era in web development, showcasing the confidence that these industry giants had in WebAssembly's capabilities.

At the heart of WebAssembly's MVP was the wasm binary format. This ground-breaking format offered a host of advantages over existing paradigms. Among them, smaller file sizes stood out as a significant benefit, making the transfer of data across the web much more efficient. Additionally, the wasm binary format was designed to be parsed at breakneck speeds, far outpacing the parsing time for equivalent JavaScript files. These combined benefits addressed some of the longstanding bottlenecks in web performance, offering both efficiency and speed.

The development community was quick to recognize the transformative potential of WebAssembly. Eager to explore and experiment, developers began to port older, legacy applications to the web. What was once a Herculean task, laden with performance issues and compatibility headaches, suddenly became dramatically more manageable. WebAssembly offered a bridge between traditional software development and the modern web, simplifying the task of bringing complex applications into a web-based environment.

The gaming industry, which is often at the forefront of adopting new technologies, was one of the first to see the enormous potential of WebAssembly. Many game developers found WebAssembly's capabilities to be a game-changer, quite literally. Leading game engines like Unity were quick to hop on the bandwagon, announcing formal support for WebAssembly. This move marked a seismic shift, empowering game developers to bring high-quality, performance-intensive games to the web without the barriers that previously stood in the way. With Unity's endorsement, the message was clear: WebAssembly was not just a theoretical concept but a practical tool capable of revolutionizing entire industries.

Broadening Horizons beyond MVP

Post its initial release, the evolution of WebAssembly was anything but stagnant:

- Threads: To harness multi-core processors' power, WebAssembly introduced support for threads, making it even more suited for performance-intensive tasks.

- Garbage Collection: Integration with the browser's garbage collector was explored, allowing languages relying on garbage collection to better interact with WebAssembly.

- ES Module Integration: This aimed to streamline the interaction between JavaScript and WebAssembly modules.

- Streaming Compilation: For even faster load times, browsers like Firefox introduced streaming compilation, where the browser compiles WebAssembly code while still downloading it.

Expanding Language Landscape

One of WebAssembly's most celebrated features is its ability to open the web to multiple languages. Initially, C and C++ were the primary languages that could be compiled to WebAssembly. However, the landscape quickly expanded. Rust, a language known for its performance and safety features, became a favored choice for WebAssembly development. Languages like Python, Go, and even .NET languages started exploring and offering WebAssembly compilation targets.

Today, WebAssembly stands not as a novelty but a staple in the web development toolkit. Its applications are vast:

- Web Games: With near-native performance, WebAssembly has revolutionized browser-based gaming.

- Education: Platforms teaching coding can now run compilers directly in the browser, thanks to WebAssembly.
- Graphics and Media Editing: Tasks like image or video editing, previously thought too intensive for the web, are now achievable.
- Scientific Simulations: WebAssembly has been instrumental in bringing complex simulations, often reserved for dedicated software, to the browser environment.
- Future Prospects

While WebAssembly has achieved much, its journey is far from over. Efforts are underway to further enhance its capabilities, from handling heavyweight desktop applications to possible server-side applications. The burgeoning field of Web3, decentralized internet, and blockchain technology also sees potential integrations with WebAssembly.

From its inception as a vision for a faster, more efficient web to its present-day applications, WebAssembly represents the epitome of collaborative innovation. It underscores the web's ever-evolving nature, reminding developers and users alike of the limitless possibilities that lie ahead. As we delve deeper into this book, you will journey through WebAssembly's multifaceted world, discovering its intricacies, tools, and transformative impact.

WebAssembly and JavaScript

WebAssembly and JavaScript, while designed to coexist harmoniously, are fundamentally different in several aspects, from their origins to their performance attributes and use cases. This analysis aims to elucidate the distinct characteristics that set WebAssembly apart from JavaScript. JavaScript was introduced in the 1990s as a scripting language for the web, specifically designed to be interpreted by browsers. Its primary function was to add interactivity to web pages. Over time, with the advent of AJAX and various frameworks, JavaScript evolved to handle more complex operations and became the backbone of modern web applications. WebAssembly, on the other hand, was introduced much later, around the mid-2010s. Its creation was motivated by the need to address performance bottlenecks that JavaScript faced in certain computationally intensive tasks. While JavaScript was text-based and interpreted, WebAssembly was designed to be a low-level binary format, compiled ahead of time.

Performance and Compilation

One of the most pronounced differences lies in how the two are processed:

- JavaScript: It's an interpreted language. When a browser encounters JavaScript, it first parses the text, then compiles it into bytecode, and finally interprets or JIT (Just-In-Time) compiles it to machine code, which is then executed. This multi-step process, especially for large scripts, can lead to delays in execution.

- WebAssembly: WASM binaries are a low-level format close to machine code. Upon loading a .wasm module, the browser can quickly convert it to machine code and execute it. The ahead-of-time compilation ensures that the performance overhead associated with interpretation is avoided.

Language Flexibility

JavaScript, as a language, is exclusive to the web platform. Developers are bound to its syntax and paradigms. However, its vast ecosystem, bolstered by libraries like React, Angular, and Vue, offers a lot of functionality and versatility. WebAssembly distinguishes itself by being language-agnostic. Instead of being a language, it's a compile target. This means developers can write code in languages like C, C++, Rust, and more, and then compile that code to WebAssembly. This opens up a wealth of opportunities, especially for developers and teams who have expertise in languages other than JavaScript and wish to leverage that for web applications.

Memory Management

JavaScript uses garbage collection for memory management. While this is convenient and reduces the potential for memory leaks, it can introduce unpredictabilities in performance, especially when dealing with real-time applications. WebAssembly, on the other hand, provides developers with explicit control over memory. While this requires a deeper understanding and meticulous management, it affords greater flexibility, especially in performance-critical scenarios.

Security and Sandboxing

Both JavaScript and WebAssembly operate within the security constraints of a browser, ensuring that malicious code cannot harm a user's system. However, their approaches differ:

- JavaScript: It runs within the JavaScript engine, which provides its sandboxing mechanism. While robust, the complexities of JavaScript's vast features can pose potential security challenges.

- WebAssembly: It operates within a stack-based virtual machine. This environment is deliberately designed to be low-level and minimalistic, reducing the surface area for potential vulnerabilities.

Interoperability with Web Platform

JavaScript has an inherent advantage when it comes to interacting with web APIs and the Document Object Model (DOM). Given that it was designed for the web, its integration is seamless. WebAssembly, in its original design, didn't have direct access to the DOM. Instead, it required intermediation through JavaScript. However, with advancements, there are ongoing efforts to provide WebAssembly with more direct ways to interact with web APIs without necessarily going through JavaScript.

Typing System

JavaScript is dynamically typed. Variables can hold values of any type, and type checking happens at runtime. While this provides flexibility, it can introduce runtime errors if types don't match expected values. WebAssembly operates on a different paradigm. It has a statically-typed system, where the types are defined at compile-time. This not only aids in performance optimizations but also provides a level of type safety.

Concurrency

Modern web applications, especially gaming or simulation platforms, benefit from parallelism. JavaScript, being single-threaded, relied on Web Workers for threading, but this approach has limitations. WebAssembly is introducing support for threads, which, combined with its performance attributes, can lead to highly responsive and concurrent web applications. Overall, while WebAssembly and JavaScript can function in tandem, they cater to different needs and possess unique characteristics. WebAssembly's introduction doesn't signify an eclipse of JavaScript; rather, it represents a broadening of possibilities, empowering developers with more tools to craft the next generation of web experiences.

Exploring WebAssembly Ecosystem

The WebAssembly (WASM) ecosystem is vast and multi-dimensional, offering a plethora of tools, frameworks, and resources. This expansive ecosystem is one of the significant reasons why WebAssembly has seen rapid adoption and continues to be an attractive platform for web developers. We shall delve into its intricacies.

Compilation Targets and Languages

At the heart of the WebAssembly ecosystem are the numerous languages that can be compiled down to WASM:

- Rust: Over time, Rust has emerged as a preferred language for WebAssembly development. With safety guarantees, concurrency features, and performance on par with C++, Rust offers a comprehensive toolkit for WASM. The wasm-bindgen tool facilitates communication between Rust and JavaScript.

- C and C++: Given their low-level nature, C and C++ were some of the first languages to be used as compilation targets for WebAssembly. Emscripten, a prominent tool in the ecosystem, allows for the conversion of C/C++ codebases into WebAssembly.

- AssemblyScript: An intriguing addition, AssemblyScript lets developers write in a language very close to TypeScript. It's designed explicitly for WebAssembly, making it an attractive option for those already familiar with JavaScript's superset.

- Other Languages: The WebAssembly landscape isn't limited to the above. Other languages, such as Kotlin, Go, and even Python, are gradually finding their way into the WebAssembly compilation framework.

Tools and Toolchains

The tools within the WebAssembly ecosystem enable efficient compilation, optimization, debugging, and integration:

- Emscripten: Beyond compiling C/C++ to WebAssembly, Emscripten offers a suite of tools, including a file system emulator and APIs for integrating with the web platform.

- Binaryen: It's a compiler and toolchain infrastructure library for WebAssembly. With components like wasm-opt for module optimization, it plays a crucial role in refining the final WASM binaries.

- WABT (WebAssembly Binary Toolkit): WABT comprises a set of utilities like wat2wasm and wasm2wat, allowing developers to convert between WebAssembly's text representation (WAT) and binary format (WASM).

- WebAssembly Explorer: An online tool, it lets developers see the resultant WebAssembly code from C/C++ sources, aiding in understanding and optimization.

Runtime Environments

While browsers are the primary execution grounds for WebAssembly, standalone runtimes extend its capabilities beyond:

- Wasmtime: A standalone JIT-style runtime for WebAssembly, Wasmtime enables WASM execution outside the browser. It's particularly useful for server-side applications.

- Wasm3: Boasting the title of the fastest WebAssembly interpreter, Wasm3 can be deployed in various environments, including embedded systems.

- Lucet: Developed by Fastly, Lucet is designed for edge computing. It can instantiate and execute WebAssembly modules in a matter of microseconds, suiting latency-sensitive applications.

Integration Frameworks

To streamline the process of integrating WebAssembly within web applications, several frameworks have arisen:

- Wasm-bindgen: Focused on the Rust-WASM ecosystem, wasm-bindgen facilitates easy communication between Rust and JavaScript, automatically generating the necessary bindings.

- Wasmer-JS: It allows WebAssembly modules to run in both Node.js and browser environments, providing a consistent API and handling aspects like module caching.

Debugging and Profiling

Ensuring robust WebAssembly applications necessitates advanced debugging and profiling tools:

- wasm-debug: A collection of utilities and libraries, wasm-debug aids in debugging WebAssembly modules, offering source-level debugging.

- Chrome DevTools: The Chrome browser has integrated WebAssembly debugging support within its DevTools. Developers can inspect and debug WASM binaries similar to JavaScript.

Package Managers and Repositories

Sharing and reusing WebAssembly modules is facilitated by package managers and repositories:

- WAPM (WebAssembly Package Manager): Acting similarly to npm for JavaScript, WAPM allows developers to publish and share their WebAssembly modules. It integrates seamlessly with Wasmer.

- pkg.wasm: A curated list of WebAssembly packages and libraries, it offers resources spanning multiple domains, from graphics to machine learning.

Community and Learning Resources

The WebAssembly community is vibrant, fostering learning and collaboration:

- Awesome WebAssembly: A curated list on GitHub, it collates numerous resources, from articles and tutorials to videos and presentations.

- WebAssembly Weekly: A newsletter that rounds up the latest developments, articles, and resources in the WASM ecosystem.

- Community Groups: Platforms like Stack Overflow, Reddit, and the W3C WebAssembly Community Group act as hubs for discussions, queries, and collaborative efforts.

The WebAssembly ecosystem is ever-evolving, with each tool, framework, and resource contributing to its versatility and power. As we venture deeper into the realm of WebAssembly in subsequent discussions, these components and their interplay will continually surface, underlining the richness and dynamism of WebAssembly's world.

Applied Usage of WebAssembly

In a very short amount of time, WebAssembly (WASM) has gone from being a novel technology to a foundational pillar in a number of different fields of modern computing. It offers a one-of-a-kind combination of portability, performance, and integration capabilities, which is the source of its widespread appeal. In the following, we will investigate some of the most prominent areas in which WebAssembly is making a discernible difference.

Web Gaming and Multimedia

WebAssembly's efficiency and performance capabilities have significantly enhanced the world of online gaming and multimedia:

- Performance Boost: WebAssembly's ability to execute code near native speed means games can now run more complex graphics, physics simulations, and AI algorithms directly in browsers. This enhances the user experience, making web games more competitive with their native counterparts.

- Unity and Unreal Engine: Renowned game development platforms, such as Unity and Unreal Engine, have adopted WebAssembly for their web exports. Developers can now create a game on these platforms and then compile it to WASM to run on the web. This seamless integration means that games previously bound to native platforms can now reach wider audiences via browsers.

- Video Editing and Streaming: WebAssembly enables on-the-fly video editing and manipulation within the browser, providing functionalities like trimming, filters, and overlays without relying on server-side processing. Furthermore, with codecs compiled to WASM, browsers can support a wider variety of video formats, enhancing streaming capabilities.

Cloud and Edge Computing

WebAssembly is revolutionizing how computation is approached at the cloud's edge:

- Server-side WASM: With standalone runtimes like Wasmtime and Lucet, WebAssembly can execute on servers, providing a sandboxed, fast-execution environment. This makes it a potential tool for microservices and serverless architectures, where quick startup times and safety are paramount.

- Edge Computing: Companies like Cloudflare and Fastly are leveraging WebAssembly for edge computing. Given WASM's compact binary format and rapid execution, computations can be moved closer to the user, reducing latency. WebAssembly modules are run in edge locations, processing data without the need to round-trip to central servers.

Image and Graphics Processing

The realm of online image and graphics manipulation has been supercharged by WebAssembly:

- ImageMagick: A renowned suite for image manipulation, ImageMagick has been ported to WebAssembly. This allows intricate image processing tasks, such as format conversion, transformations, and effects, to be conducted directly within the browser.

- CAD and 3D Modeling: WebAssembly facilitates browser-based CAD tools and 3D modeling applications, previously limited due to computational constraints. Users can now interact with complex 3D models, run simulations, and even design components without installing hefty native software.

Scientific Computing and Simulations

WebAssembly's performance attributes make it fit for scientific computations:

- Molecular Modeling and Simulations: Tools that model molecular structures and run chemical simulations can benefit from the efficient computation that WebAssembly offers. By leveraging WASM, researchers and students can visualize and manipulate complex molecular structures directly in web applications.

- Data Analysis and Visualization: Scientific datasets, often voluminous and intricate, can be processed and visualized in the browser using tools compiled to WebAssembly. This democratizes access to data analysis, allowing researchers from diverse domains to interact with and glean insights from data without relying on standalone software.

Cryptography and Security

WebAssembly plays an instrumental role in online security practices:

- Cryptography Libraries: Cryptographic operations, essential for tasks like data encryption, hashing, and digital signatures, demand robust computational prowess. Several cryptographic libraries, previously available only for native applications, have been ported to WebAssembly, facilitating high-speed cryptographic operations directly in browsers.

- Blockchain and Smart Contracts: The blockchain realm, especially platforms that support smart contracts, is exploring WebAssembly. Ethereum, one of the largest blockchain platforms, is considering WASM as an execution method for its smart contracts. Given WebAssembly's deterministic nature, it can ensure consistent contract execution across nodes.

The applications of WebAssembly span a broad spectrum. From enhancing web interactivity through games and multimedia to bolstering scientific research, cloud computing, and securing online interactions, WebAssembly's impact is profound. As the technology matures, and as the ecosystem around it grows richer, it's evident that its influence will only permeate deeper into diverse computing domains.

Key Concepts and Terminologies

Modules

Definition

A WebAssembly module is a binary representation of a program or a part of a program. It's the unit of deployment, compilation, and caching in WebAssembly.

Characteristics

Modules are stateless and side-effect-free. They define types, imports, functions, tables, memories, and exports. Once compiled, a module results in a WebAssembly instance, which can be invoked and interacted with.

Memories

Definition

Memories in WebAssembly refer to resizable arrays of bytes, which act as the linear memory used by the module's functions.

Characteristics

The WebAssembly memory model supports direct load/store operations. These memories can be shared between WebAssembly modules and JavaScript, enabling efficient data transfer without copying.

Tables

Definition

WebAssembly tables are resizable typed arrays of references (not bytes). These can be considered somewhat analogous to arrays in high-level languages.

Usage

Initially, tables were introduced to provide a way to store and manipulate function references, but their utility has expanded. They facilitate indirect function calls and can even store references to other WebAssembly constructs.

Imports and Exports

Definition

Imports are entities (like functions, memories, or tables) that a WebAssembly module expects to be provided from its environment. Exports, on the other hand, are entities the module makes available to its environment.

Purpose

By defining strict boundaries of interaction through imports and exports, WebAssembly ensures modularity. This also facilitates clear communication between WebAssembly and its host environment (like JavaScript).

WebAssembly Text Format (WAT)

Definition

WAT is a human-readable representation of WebAssembly modules. While the binary format (WASM) is what runs, WAT helps developers write, read, and debug.

Characteristics

WAT has a s-expression syntax. Tools like wasm2wat and wat2wasm from the WABT toolkit enable easy conversion between binary and text formats.

Stack Machines and Operations

Definition

WebAssembly is designed around a stack machine rather than a register machine. This means its operations work on a last-in-first-out (LIFO) data structure, where results are pushed onto the stack, and operations pop their inputs from the stack.

Significance

Stack-based architectures simplify the WebAssembly design, make for a smaller binary format, and allow for straightforward decoding and validation.

Validation

Definition

Before any WebAssembly code is executed, it's validated to ensure safety and correctness.

Characteristics

The validation process checks various aspects, such as ensuring the code respects the WebAssembly types and doesn't access memory out of bounds. This step is crucial for security and reliability.

WebAssembly JavaScript API

Definition

The WebAssembly JavaScript API provides a structured way for JavaScript to interact with WebAssembly.

Functions

This API allows JavaScript to compile and instantiate WebAssembly modules, access WebAssembly functions, and interact with WebAssembly memory, among other operations.

Opcode

Definition

Opcodes, or operation codes, are the elementary operations that WebAssembly can perform.

Variety
WebAssembly provides a variety of opcodes, from basic arithmetic and control flow operations to memory access and type conversion operations.

Start Function

Definition
A WebAssembly module can have a designated start function, which is automatically executed when the module is instantiated.

Usage
This is beneficial for initialization routines that should run before any other part of the module.

WebAssembly Threads

Definition
Threads in WebAssembly represent the concept of parallel execution of tasks. Through the introduction of shared memories and atomic operations, WebAssembly threads enable concurrent programming.

Characteristics
With WebAssembly threads, shared memory is allowed, meaning multiple WebAssembly instances (or workers) can read and write to a single memory concurrently. Atomic operations ensure that specific sequences of operations are completed without interruption, guaranteeing data consistency.

WebAssembly Core Specification

Definition
This is the formal document that defines the WebAssembly standard. It provides the exact semantics, binary format, and execution details of WebAssembly.

Purpose
By having a well-defined core specification, it ensures consistency across different WebAssembly implementations and allows developers to have a consistent set of expectations.

Host Functions

Definition
Host functions are functions provided by the host environment, such as the browser or a standalone runtime, which can be called by a WebAssembly module.

Usage
These functions allow WebAssembly modules to interact with their surroundings, enabling operations like DOM manipulation or network requests when running in a browser context.

Structured Control Flow

Definition
This refers to WebAssembly's approach to control flow, where constructs like loops and conditionals are structured strictly to avoid complexities and improve optimization.

Advantages
This design choice simplifies the task for compilers and makes the generated code more predictable and easier to optimize.

WebAssembly's Embedding in HTML

Definition
WebAssembly can be embedded directly within HTML documents, similar to how JavaScript can be embedded.

Integration
By using the <script type='module'> tag with the appropriate MIME type (application/wasm), developers can directly integrate WebAssembly modules into web pages. This enables seamless interactions between HTML, JavaScript, and WebAssembly.

Traps

Definition
Traps in WebAssembly are runtime errors that halt the execution of the program.

Examples
Common situations where traps might occur include division by zero, integer overflow, or accessing out-of-bounds memory. When such an error is detected, WebAssembly ensures that execution stops, thus maintaining the integrity and safety of the environment.

These above concepts and various terminologies further deepen our understanding of WebAssembly's design philosophy and its interaction mechanisms with the broader ecosystem.

Understanding Architecture of WebAssembly

WebAssembly's architecture is grounded in its design principles of being fast, secure, and platform-independent. It's architected as a low-level virtual machine that runs code at near-native speed, making it apt for both web and server applications. To understand its architecture, we need to delve into its components and their interactions.

Virtual Stack Machine Design

At its core, WebAssembly operates as a virtual stack machine. This means that instead of relying on physical registers, WebAssembly uses a stack to perform its operations. The virtual stack machine design aids in the following:

- Compactness: The stack-based design leads to a concise binary format, reducing the size of WebAssembly files, hence faster downloads.

- Efficient Decoding: Stack-based representations are straightforward to decode and convert into native machine instructions.

- Portability: The abstraction provided by the stack ensures that WebAssembly can be easily ported across various architectures.

Binary Format (WASM)

The WASM format is the binary representation of WebAssembly modules. It's designed for compactness and efficiency. The key facets include:

- Sections: WASM files are divided into sections such as type, function, global, and more. Each section has a specific role, like defining function signatures or declaring imported functions.

- Immediate Values and Endianness: WASM uses immediate values (constants) directly in its instructions and adheres to little-endian format, ensuring consistent representation across platforms.

Linear Memory

WebAssembly's memory model is a contiguous, resizable array of bytes known as linear memory. This is the primary means by which data storage and manipulation occur.

- Isolation: For security, WebAssembly's linear memory is isolated from the host's memory. Interactions between them occur through explicit operations.

- Growth: While the memory is fixed at instantiation, it can grow during execution to accommodate dynamic data needs, but it can never shrink.

Structured Control Flow

WebAssembly uses a structured control flow mechanism, avoiding complexities like arbitrary jumps, which can lead to unpredictable behavior.

WebAssembly has block constructs that allow for the creation of nested lexical scopes. These blocks can be used to create loops, conditionals, and other control flow structures.

Security and Sandboxing

One of WebAssembly's pivotal architectural components is its commitment to security.

- Validation: Before execution, WebAssembly code undergoes rigorous validation checks to ensure it adheres to safety rules.

- Sandboxing: WebAssembly runs inside a sandboxed environment, ensuring that even if malicious code is executed, it can't harm the host system.

JavaScript Interface

Although WebAssembly is designed to work alongside JavaScript, the interface between them is clearly defined.

- APIs: WebAssembly provides JavaScript APIs that allow for tasks such as compiling, instantiating, and interacting with WebAssembly modules from JavaScript.

- Data Transfer: Complex data structures cannot be passed directly between WebAssembly and JavaScript. Instead, they are usually passed by reference or transformed into simpler structures that both understand.

Threads and Concurrency

With the advent of WebAssembly threads, the architecture now supports parallelism.

- Shared Memory: WebAssembly threads can share linear memories, allowing for true parallelism as multiple workers operate on the same memory concurrently.

- Atomics: Atomic operations ensure that certain sequences of operations on shared memory occur without interruption, guaranteeing data consistency in a concurrent environment.

Embedding

While the most common host environment for WebAssembly is the web browser, it's designed to be host-agnostic.

- Browsers: In browsers, WebAssembly is embedded within the larger web ecosystem, allowing it to interact with the DOM, WebGL, Web Audio, and more.

- Non-web Embeddings: WebAssembly can also be embedded in non-web environments such as standalone runtimes (e.g., WASI) or server-side platforms, broadening its range of applications.

To wrap it up, WebAssembly's architecture is a blend of efficiency, security, and versatility. The components seamlessly interact, ensuring that WebAssembly modules run quickly and safely, irrespective of the host environment.

Summary

WebAssembly, often abbreviated as WASM, stands as a ground-breaking advancement in the realm of web development. Initially, the web landscape was predominantly ruled by JavaScript, which, despite its versatility, had limitations in terms of performance and applicability for high-end computational tasks. WebAssembly emerged as a solution, providing a binary instruction format that acts as a virtual machine, offering near-native performance for web applications. Delving into its architectural nuances, WebAssembly is built upon the foundational concept of a virtual stack machine. This design choice, inherently different from traditional register-based machines, grants WebAssembly compactness and efficiency, both crucial for swift web-based operations. The WASM binary format, a compact representation of WebAssembly modules, is structured meticulously with delineated sections such as function, type, and global. These sections house specific information, ensuring organized and efficient execution. Accompanying this is WebAssembly's linear memory model, a continuous resizable byte array. This model, while being the primary data storage mechanism, is isolated from the host's memory, signifying the platform's commitment to security.

WebAssembly doesn't just stop at ensuring security through memory isolation. Before any WebAssembly code meets execution, it undergoes rigorous validation processes, ensuring adherence to safety protocols. Moreover, the sandboxed environment in which it operates serves as an additional layer of protection against potential malicious intents. But WebAssembly isn't an isolated entity; it's designed to operate harmoniously with JavaScript. Through well-defined APIs, WebAssembly can be compiled, instantiated, and even interacted with, all from within JavaScript. This symbiotic relationship extends beyond just JavaScript. WebAssembly's architecture is inherently agnostic to its host environment. While browsers remain its primary habitat, WebAssembly's adaptability allows it to thrive in non-web environments too, such as standalone runtimes or server-side platforms. A particularly noteworthy feature of WebAssembly is its support for threads and concurrency. With shared linear memories, multiple workers can operate simultaneously on the same memory. Coupled with atomic operations, WebAssembly ensures data consistency, even in a high-concurrency scenario. Such features, combined with its compatibility with various tools and languages, position WebAssembly as a transformative force in web development, unlocking a spectrum of possibilities previously unattainable.

CHAPTER 2: FUNDAMENTALS OF WEBASSEMBLY PROGRAMMING

WebAssembly Text Format (WAT)

WebAssembly, as an instrumental pivot in web development, provides two distinct formats: the binary format (WASM) and the text format (WAT). While the binary format serves as a compact representation designed for swift execution and transfer, the text format acts as its readable counterpart, beneficial for debugging, understanding, and manual editing. We shall dissect the world of WAT and its juxtaposition with the binary format.

What is WebAssembly Text Format (WAT)?

WAT stands for WebAssembly Text, which is the human-readable representation of WebAssembly's binary format. Think of it as the assembly language for WebAssembly's virtual machine. It allows developers to write, read, or modify WebAssembly code in a more intuitive manner, similar to how assembly languages operate for traditional computer architectures. A standard WAT module showcases the module's functions, types, imports, exports, and other elements using s-expressions, a notation that originates from the Lisp programming language. S-expressions use nested parentheses to represent hierarchical data, making the code structure evident.

Dichotomy of Binary vs. Text Format

Representation

- Binary (WASM): It's a compact, machine-readable format, encoded in bytes. This encoding is not directly readable by humans but is optimized for size and speed, ensuring quick loading times and swift execution.

- Text (WAT): This format is a linear, textual representation of a module's structure, using the aforementioned s-expressions. Unlike the byte-coded binary, WAT is directly readable and writable by developers.

Purpose & Utility

- Binary: Its compact nature makes it apt for transmission over the internet. As browsers fetch this binary format, the minimized size ensures reduced download times, benefiting web applications' performance.

- Text: The legibility of WAT promotes debugging, manual code edits, and provides an avenue for developers to understand WebAssembly's inner workings. It's predominantly a medium for development and is typically not used in production.

- Conversion: Between the two formats, conversion is seamless. Tools like wat2wasm and wasm2wat facilitate the transformation of WAT to binary and vice versa. This bi-directional conversion ensures that developers can switch between the formats based on the task at hand.

Anatomy & Syntax

- Binary: The binary format, with its byte-coded nature, contains sections like type, function, and global. Each section possesses a specific role, ensuring an organized execution flow.

- Text: WAT, with its s-expression-based syntax, mirrors the structure of the binary but in a verbose manner. For instance, while defining a function in WAT, one might use (func ...), with parameters and instructions nested within.

Practical Insights into WAT

To visualize the difference, consider a simple WebAssembly function that adds two numbers. In the binary format, it would be a series of bytes, not discernible at a glance. However, in WAT, it might look something like:

```
(module
  (func $add (param $a i32) (param $b i32) (result i32)
    get_local $a
    get_local $b
    i32.add)
)
```

The textual representation elucidates the function's intent, parameters, and the operation. Here, $add is a function that takes two 32-bit integers (i32) as parameters and returns their sum.

WebAssembly Text Format, or WAT, emerges as an indispensable tool in the WebAssembly ecosystem, especially for developers aiming to delve deeper into the mechanics of WebAssembly. While the binary format remains the champion for web deployment due to its compactness and efficiency, WAT provides the clarity and transparency often sought during development phases. It embodies the philosophy that, while machines crave efficiency, humans desire understanding, and through WAT, WebAssembly caters to both.

WebAssembly Data Types

At the core of any programming paradigm, be it high-level languages or assembly-like formats such as WebAssembly, are data types. These typifications determine the nature of data that can be stored and processed. In WebAssembly, the data type repertoire is intentionally kept compact, focusing on efficiency and cross-platform compatibility. We shall navigate through these types and observe them in practical scenarios.

Basic Numeric Types

i32

Represents a 32-bit integer. Given its range, it can store numbers from -2,147,483,648 to 2,147,483,647.

Example: Storing and adding two numbers.

```
(module
  (func $add_two_nums (param $a i32) (param $b i32) (result i32)
    get_local $a
    get_local $b
    i32.add)
)
```

i64

Embodies a 64-bit integer. It caters to much larger numbers, ranging from -9,223,372,036,854,775,808 to 9,223,372,036,854,775,807.

Example: Multiplying two large numbers.

```
(module
  (func $multiply_large_nums (param $x i64) (param $y i64) (result i64)
    get_local $x
    get_local $y
    i64.mul)
)
```

f32

Stands for 32-bit floating-point numbers. Essential for decimal value calculations.

Example: Calculating the division of two floats.

```
(module
  (func $divide_floats (param $m f32) (param $n f32) (result f32)
    get_local $m
    get_local $n
    f32.div)
)
```

f64

A 64-bit floating-point number. This data type is more precise than f32, catering to applications demanding higher precision.

Example: Finding the square root of a number.

```
(module
  (func $sqrt_num (param $val f64) (result f64)
    get_local $val
    f64.sqrt)
)
```

Memory

WebAssembly operates with a linear memory model, represented as an array of bytes. Each module can have a memory associated, which can be imported, exported, and manipulated via instructions.

Example: Allocating and initializing memory.

```
(module
  (memory $myMemory 1) ; Allocating 1 memory page (64KiB)
  (data (i32.const 0) "Hello, Wasm!") ; Initializing memory with a string
)
```

Table

A table in WebAssembly is an array of references, not of raw bytes like memory. Currently, it is predominantly used for function references, aiding in indirect function calls.

Example: Declaring a table and calling a function indirectly.

```
(module
  (type $fn_type (func (param i32) (result i32)))
  (table $myTable 1 anyfunc) ; Table of size 1 holding any function reference
  (elem (i32.const 0) $sample_function) ; Initializing table with a function reference
  (func $sample_function (param $p i32) (result i32)
    get_local $p
    i32.const 1
    i32.add)
  (func $call_indirectly (param $index i32) (param $value i32) (result i32)
    get_local $value
    get_local $index
    call_indirect $fn_type)
)
```

Global

Globals are variables that are accessible throughout the WebAssembly module. They can hold values of i32, i64, f32, or f64 types.

Example: Defining and using a global variable.

```
(module
  (global $g (mut i32) (i32.const 10)) ; Defining a mutable global of type i32 initialized to
10
  (func $increment_global
    get_global $g
    i32.const 1
    i32.add
    set_global $g)
)
```

Type

Though not a data type in the traditional sense, the type construct in WebAssembly lets developers define abstract function types. This becomes crucial for creating tables of function references or defining function signatures.

Example: Defining a function type and using it.

```
(module
  (type $fn_signature (func (param i32) (result i32)))
  (func $sample (type $fn_signature)
    i32.const 42)
)
```

In essence, WebAssembly's data types, though compact, offer a vast landscape of computational possibilities. Through their strategic implementation and combination, they form the bedrock on which powerful web applications are constructed, championing performance, precision, and adaptability.

Variables: Creation, Usage, and Its Scope

Variables, both in high-level languages and low-level representations such as WebAssembly, are crucial in facilitating data storage and manipulation. These elements act as containers, holding values or references to them. Understanding how WebAssembly handles variables is pivotal for anyone aiming to grasp the system's nuances.

Local Variables

In WebAssembly, local variables, often simply referred to as "locals," reside within a specific function's scope. They get initialized when the function is called and are discarded when the function exits. Declaration and Initialization: Local variables can be declared with or without an initial value. Their types must be specified upon declaration. WebAssembly currently supports i32, i64, f32, and f64 as local variable types.

Example: Declaring two local variables.

```
(module
  (func $sum_two_numbers (param $a i32) (param $b i32) (result i32)
    (local $localA i32) ; Declaring without initial value
    (local $localB i32 (i32.const 20)) ; Declaring with initial value
    get_local $a
    get_local $b
    i32.add)
)
```

Accessing and Manipulating Local Variables

Local variables can be read using the get_local instruction and modified using the set_local instruction.

Example: Modifying a local variable's value.

```
(module
  (func $increment_by_one (param $num i32) (result i32)
    (local $result i32)
    get_local $num
    i32.const 1
    i32.add
    set_local $result
    get_local $result)
)
```

Global Variables

As the name implies, global variables have module-wide scope. This means they're accessible from any function within the module. Their primary purpose is to maintain state across function calls. Declaration and Initialization: Just like locals, globals must be declared with a type. However, unlike locals, they can be mutable (mut) or immutable. This mutability determines if the global's value can be changed during execution.

Example: Declaring a mutable global variable.

```
(module
  (global $counter (mut i32) (i32.const 0))
  (func $increment_counter
    get_global $counter
    i32.const 1
    i32.add
    set_global $counter)
)
```

Accessing and Manipulating Global Variables

Reading and writing to global variables is analogous to locals, using the get_global and set_global instructions, respectively.

Example: Reading a global variable.

```
(module
  (global $data (mut i32) (i32.const 100))
  (func $get_data_value (result i32)
    get_global $data)
)
```

The primary difference between locals and globals, besides their accessibility, is their lifetime. Local variables come into existence when their parent function is invoked and disappear once it exits. On the contrary, global variables persist for the module's entire lifetime. To sum up, variables in WebAssembly, be it local or global, serve as the foundational blocks enabling complex computations and logic flow. Their management, while being slightly different from traditional high-level languages, is streamlined and efficient, keeping in line with WebAssembly's design principles of speed and compactness.

Control Structures

Control structures are pivotal for orchestrating the flow of program execution. They empower developers to implement logic branches, loops, and jumps that enable the creation of dynamic applications. In WebAssembly (Wasm), control structures might be reminiscent of those in traditional programming languages but have unique nuances.

Basic Structured Flow

The foundational element of WebAssembly's control structures is the block. A block groups a sequence of instructions, permitting a single entry point and a single exit point.

Practical Demonstration

```
(module
  (func $simple_block
    (block
      i32.const 10
```

```
      drop  ; this will drop the constant 10 from the stack
    )
  )
)
```

This above sample snippet demonstrates a block with a constant integer and a drop operation. The drop instruction discards the topmost value of the operand stack.

Conditional Execution with if and else

Conditional statements, such as if and else, allow branching based on evaluations.

Practical Demonstration

```
(module
  (func $is_even (param $n i32) (result i32)
    get_local $n
    i32.const 2
    i32.rem_u  ; remainder after division
    (if (result i32)
      (then i32.const 0)  ; if remainder is 0, number is even
      (else i32.const 1)  ; else, number is odd
    )
  )
)
```

In this snippet, we determine if a number is even or odd. The function returns 0 for even numbers and 1 for odd.

Loops

WebAssembly's loop provides a way to execute a block of code repeatedly. Unlike traditional loops, a Wasm loop doesn't have a built-in condition check. Instead, you use other control instructions inside the loop to dictate when to break out.

Practical Demonstration

```
(module
  (func $count_to_n (param $n i32) (result i32)
    (local $counter i32 (i32.const 0))
    (loop
      get_local $counter
      get_local $n
      i32.ge_s   ; checks if counter >= n
      (if
        (then br 1)  ; if true, break out of the loop
      )
      get_local $counter
      i32.const 1
      i32.add
      set_local $counter
      br 0  ; go back to the beginning of the loop
    )
    get_local $counter
  )
)
```

Here, we've crafted a simple counting function. It counts from 0 up to (and including) n, illustrating how you might emulate a for-loop in WebAssembly.

Nested Blocks and Scoping

Blocks can nest inside other blocks or control constructs, leading to the concept of scopes. In Wasm, each block, loop, or if construct has its own scope, which can be targeted using the br instruction followed by the depth of the target.

Practical Demonstration

```
(module
  (func $nested_blocks
    (block
      (block
        i32.const 5
```

```
            br 1  ; this breaks out of both blocks, targeting the outer one
        )
        ; this code won't execute due to the branch above
        i32.const 10
        drop
      )
    )
  )
```

In the above module, the inner block contains a branch that exits both the inner and outer blocks.

The br_if and br_table Instructions

br_if performs a conditional branch. If the top of the stack is non-zero, it branches to a target; otherwise, it continues with the next instruction. br_table is used for table jumps, akin to a switch-case mechanism.

Practical Demonstration

```
(module
  (func $evaluate (param $x i32) (result i32)
    get_local $x
    (br_table
      (case 0 i32.const 100)
      (case 1 i32.const 200)
      (case 2 i32.const 300)
      (default i32.const 400)  ; default case
    )
  )
)
```

Here, based on the input value of x, different constants are returned, showcasing a switch-like mechanism. Through this exploration, it's evident that while WebAssembly's control structures carry some similarities to those in traditional high-level languages, they bring unique intricacies. Their structured nature offers predictability in code execution flow, emphasizing WebAssembly's design focus on safety and efficiency.

Functions and Parameters

In the realm of programming, functions serve as modular units of reusable code. They encapsulate logic, can be invoked numerous times, and are paramount for creating structured and maintainable software. WebAssembly (Wasm) hones in on this modularity, offering a robust system for defining and invoking functions. This session dives into functions in WebAssembly, their parameters, and practical demonstrations of their utility.

Functions in WebAssembly are declared using the func keyword within a module. Each function can have zero or more parameters and can optionally return a value. The data types of both the parameters and the return values need to be explicitly declared.

Declaring and Defining Functions

A function declaration in Wasm outlines the function's signature - its parameters and return types. The definition, meanwhile, contains the actual instructions or operations that the function will execute.

Practical Demonstration

```
(module
  ;; Declaration and Definition of a function that adds two integers
  (func $add (param $a i32) (param $b i32) (result i32)
    get_local $a
    get_local $b
    i32.add
  )
)
```

In this module, we've defined a function $add that accepts two 32-bit integers, $a and $b, and returns their sum.

Invoking Functions

To utilize a function, it must be invoked or called. In Wasm, functions can be called from within other functions. Additionally, to facilitate testing and interaction from outside the module, functions can be exported, allowing them to be called externally.

Practical Demonstration

```
(module
  (func $add (param $a i32) (param $b i32) (result i32)
    get_local $a
    get_local $b
    i32.add
  )

  (func $demo_invoke
    i32.const 5
    i32.const 3
    call $add  ;; This will push the result 8 onto the stack
    drop       ;; Drop the result as it's not used further in this function
  )

  (export "addTwoNumbers" (func $add))
)
```

Here, the $demo_invoke function demonstrates how to invoke the $add function. Furthermore, $add is exported as addTwoNumbers, allowing it to be called from outside the Wasm module.

Multiple Parameters and Return Types

WebAssembly functions can accept multiple parameters and can even return multiple values, thanks to Wasm's multi-value proposal. This elevates the expressive power of functions in Wasm.

Practical Demonstration

```
(module
  ;; A function that swaps two integers and returns both
  (func $swap (param $x i32) (param $y i32) (result i32 i32)
    get_local $y
    get_local $x
  )
)
```

The $swap function accepts two integers, $x and $y, and returns them in the reverse order.

Local Variables in Functions

Beyond parameters, functions in Wasm can also declare local variables. These are function-scoped and can be utilized to store intermediate values.

Practical Demonstration

```
(module
  ;; A function that calculates the average of two integers
  (func $average (param $a i32) (param $b i32) (result i32)
    get_local $a
    get_local $b
    i32.add
    (local $sum i32)      ;; Declare a local variable
    set_local $sum        ;; Set the sum into the local variable
    get_local $sum
    i32.const 2
    i32.div_s
  )
)
```

This function calculates the average of two integers using a local variable $sum to store their sum. Functions form the heart of computational logic in WebAssembly. With parameters allowing for input flexibility and local variables granting intermediate storage, they furnish the tools to craft intricate algorithms. WebAssembly's modular design around functions ensures efficient, structured, and reusable code, vital for building complex web applications.

Memory Management

A robust memory management system is pivotal in the world of programming, as it provides the infrastructure to store and manipulate data effectively. In WebAssembly, memory is represented as a contiguous, resizable array of bytes, akin to a virtual machine's linear memory model. This linear memory is central to WebAssembly's operations, enabling data storage and interoperation with the outside world, especially with JavaScript.

WebAssembly's memory is linear, starting at address 0 and extending up. Think of it as a large array of bytes. Each module can have at most one memory instance, but this memory can be shared among multiple modules, facilitating shared data.

Declaring Memory

To utilize memory, it must be declared within a module. The declaration specifies the initial size and, optionally, a maximum size.

Practical Demonstration

```
(module
  (memory (export "mem") 1)  ;; Declare memory with an initial size of 1 page (64KiB)
)
```

Here, the module exports its memory as "mem" and initializes it with 1 page. Each page in WebAssembly is 64KiB.

Memory Resizing

WebAssembly memory can be resized, allowing for dynamic adjustments based on an application's needs. This is done using built-in operations grow_memory and current_memory.

Practical Demonstration

```
(module
  (memory 1 2)  ;; Memory with an initial size of 1 page and maximum of 2 pages

  (func $check_current_memory (result i32)
    current_memory   ;; Returns the current memory size in pages
  )

  (func $grow_by_one_page
    i32.const 1      ;; Specify by how many pages to grow
    grow_memory      ;; Grow the memory
  )
)
```

In the above sample program, $check_current_memory retrieves the current memory size, while $grow_by_one_page grows the memory by 1 page.

Memory Access

Accessing memory involves reading from or writing to specific addresses. WebAssembly provides a set of load and store instructions for various data types.

Practical Demonstration

```
(module
  (memory 1)
  (func $store_and_load
    ;; Store the number 42 at address 0
    i32.const 0      ;; Address
    i32.const 42     ;; Value
    i32.store

    ;; Load the number from address 0
    i32.const 0
    i32.load
  )
)
```

The function $store_and_load first stores the integer 42 at address 0 and then loads it back.

Memory and JavaScript Interoperation

One of WebAssembly's strengths is its ability to seamlessly interoperate with JavaScript. Shared memory makes this interaction efficient.

Practical Demonstration

```
// Instantiate the WebAssembly module
WebAssembly.instantiateStreaming(fetch('module.wasm'))
.then(result => {
  const { memory } = result.instance.exports;
```

```
  // Create a new Uint8Array backed by the WebAssembly memory
  const arr = new Uint8Array(memory.buffer, 0, 10);

  // Set the first byte to 65 ('A' in ASCII)
  arr[0] = 65;
});
```

In this JavaScript example, we instantiate a WebAssembly module and interact with its memory. We create a Uint8Array that shares the memory buffer, allowing for efficient data sharing.

Memory Safety

While the linear memory model is powerful, it requires caution. WebAssembly provides strong isolation guarantees, ensuring that even if an application tries to access out-of-bounds memory, it won't affect other parts of the system.

Data Segments

To initialize memory with constant values, WebAssembly supports data segments. These segments are part of the module and can be used to set up the memory layout with predefined data.

Practical Demonstration

```
(module
  (memory 1)
  (data (i32.const 0) "Hello, World!")
)
```

Here, the memory gets initialized with the string "Hello, World!" starting from address 0. Memory management is a cornerstone of WebAssembly, permitting sophisticated data operations and facilitating efficient collaboration with JavaScript.

Modules for Web's Computation

When we delve into the world of WebAssembly, the term 'module' frequently emerges as a cornerstone. In WebAssembly, a module is akin to a compiled binary, encapsulating both code and data. They serve as the primary means of organization and encapsulation, enabling modularization and reuse. In the broader context of software design, modularization has always been recognized as a method to improve manageability, reusability, and scalability. WebAssembly takes this principle and applies it directly within its design.

Essence of WebAssembly Module

At the most fundamental level, a WebAssembly module serves as a robust encapsulation unit for WebAssembly code along with its accompanying static data. This modular design is crucial for high-performance, readable, and maintainable code. The primary components that make up a WebAssembly module contribute to its versatility, allowing it to seamlessly interact with various web technologies and programming languages. Each part has a unique role, serving as a building block in the larger structural framework of the module. We shall dissect each component in more detail:

Functions

Functions are the elemental units of operation or logic within a WebAssembly module. They encapsulate specific tasks, calculations, or procedures that the module is designed to perform. This encapsulation not only improves code maintainability but also allows for greater flexibility and reusability. Functions can be easily invoked from within other parts of the module, or even from external JavaScript code through bindings, contributing to the module's functionality and interoperability.

Globals

In the world of WebAssembly, Globals represent a set of variables that maintain their state or values across different function calls within the same module. Unlike local variables that lose their data once a function execution is completed, Globals are persistent and thus offer a way to share data or state between various functions. This makes them an invaluable tool for achieving long-lasting state management in your applications.

Tables

Tables are a more abstract concept but play a vital role in WebAssembly modules by providing indirect references to functions. They serve as a mapping mechanism between indexes and actual function calls, enabling features like dynamic dispatch or virtual function invocations. Tables enhance the module's ability to manage function pointers, allowing you to invoke functions dynamically and even implement complex programming paradigms like object-oriented programming.

Memory

Memory, as previously elaborated, is a linear data structure that is accessed by WebAssembly functions to read and write data. This memory model enables fine-grained control over how data is stored and manipulated, which is crucial for optimizing performance. This memory space is separate from the JavaScript runtime, yet it can be accessed from JavaScript, thereby offering a secure and efficient mechanism for data storage and retrieval.

Exports and Imports

Exports and Imports form the interface of a WebAssembly module, allowing it to communicate with the outside world. Exports enable functions, variables, and other components to be made accessible outside the module, allowing for integration with JavaScript or other WebAssembly modules. On the other hand, Imports let a module pull in external functionalities, such as JavaScript functions or even other WebAssembly modules, thus expanding its capabilities beyond what is natively available within the module itself.

Creation of a WebAssembly Module

The creation of a WebAssembly module starts with the foundational step of taking source code written in high-level programming languages—commonly C, C++, or Rust—and translating it into WebAssembly bytecode. This translation process is far more than a mere conversion; it involves complex operations such as lexical analysis, parsing, and code optimization. Specialized tools like Emscripten for C and C++ or the native Rust compiler are used to undertake this compilation process effectively.

Upon successful compilation, a .wasm file is generated. This file serves as the WebAssembly module and encapsulates the logic and functionalities of the original code in a format that is optimized for speedy loading and execution. The .wasm file is not just a binary blob; it's a well-structured format that includes both the compiled code and essential metadata that facilitate efficient execution. This includes information like function signatures, local and global variables, and memory instructions among other things.

WebAssembly Module Imports and Exports

A defining feature of modules is their ability to interoperate with their environment, typically JavaScript in web scenarios. This is achieved through two mechanisms:

Consider the following simple module:

```
(module
  ;; Import a function from an external module
  (import "external" "importedFunction" (func $importedFunction))

  ;; Export a function
```

```
  (func (export "exportedFunction")
    ...
    call $importedFunction
    ...
  )
)
```

Here, the module imports a function named importedFunction from an "external" module and also exports a function named exportedFunction.

Instantiation of WebAssembly Module

Once a module is loaded, it must be instantiated to produce an instance. An instance is an in-memory representation of a module, with its own state and memory.

In a web environment, instantiation typically involves WebAssembly's JavaScript API.

Practical Demonstration

```
// Fetch and instantiate the module
WebAssembly.instantiateStreaming(fetch('module.wasm'))
.then(result => {
  // Access the module's exports
  const { exportedFunction } = result.instance.exports;
  exportedFunction();
});
```

This JavaScript snippet fetches a WebAssembly module, instantiates it, and then calls an exported function.

Bytecode and Textual Representation

While the typical distribution format for WebAssembly modules is binary bytecode, there's also a textual format (often with a .wat extension). This human-readable format is useful for debugging, learning, and occasionally hand-editing.

Practical Demonstration

Consider a simple WebAssembly module in textual format:

```
(module
  (func (export "add") (param $x i32) (param $y i32) (result i32)
    get_local $x
    get_local $y
    i32.add
  )
)
```

This module exports a function add that takes two 32-bit integers and returns their sum.

WebAssembly Arithmetic

In this section, you will harness the knowledge acquired about WebAssembly and apply it to design a basic program to perform arithmetic operations: addition, subtraction, multiplication, and division. This program will serve as our foundational example that you will expand upon throughout the book.

Setting Base

Remember the WASM textual format? You will be using that for clarity, although in practice, you'd likely use a higher-level language like C or Rust and then compile it to WebAssembly binary format.

Our Base Module: Arithmetic Operations

```
(module
  ;; Addition Function
  (func (export "add") (param $x i32) (param $y i32) (result i32)
    get_local $x
    get_local $y
    i32.add
  )

  ;; Subtraction Function
  (func (export "subtract") (param $x i32) (param $y i32) (result i32)
```

```
        get_local $x
        get_local $y
        i32.sub
    )

    ;; Multiplication Function
    (func (export "multiply") (param $x i32) (param $y i32) (result i32)
        get_local $x
        get_local $y
        i32.mul
    )

    ;; Division Function
    (func (export "divide") (param $x i32) (param $y i32) (result i32)
        get_local $x
        get_local $y
        i32.div_s
    )
)
```

This module comprises four exported functions, each corresponding to an arithmetic operation. The functions utilize 32-bit integers (i32) as input and return types. Notice how we make use of get_local to access the function parameters, and then the arithmetic operations like i32.add, i32.sub, etc.

Loading Module

With our WebAssembly module ready, we shall see how to integrate it into a web environment using JavaScript.

```
async function loadWasmModule() {
    const response = await fetch('arithmetic.wasm');
    const buffer = await response.arrayBuffer();
    const moduleObject = await WebAssembly.compile(buffer);
    const instance = await WebAssembly.instantiate(moduleObject);
```

```
  return instance.exports;
}

async function performArithmetic() {
  const wasmExports = await loadWasmModule();

  console.log("Addition: ", wasmExports.add(10, 5));       // 15
  console.log("Subtraction: ", wasmExports.subtract(10, 5)); // 5
  console.log("Multiplication: ", wasmExports.multiply(10, 5)); // 50
  console.log("Division: ", wasmExports.divide(10, 5));     // 2
}

performArithmetic();
```

Here, we asynchronously load our arithmetic.wasm module, instantiate it, and then use the exported arithmetic functions to perform operations.

This simple arithmetic program serves as a foundation. As we progress through the chapters, you will evolve this base, integrating advanced features, exploring optimizations, and demonstrating how WebAssembly interplays with other web technologies.

For instance, in upcoming chapters:

- We might expand our operations to work with floating-point numbers.
- We could optimize arithmetic operations for performance.
- You will interface more complexly with JavaScript, perhaps building a user interface.
- Dive into memory management by maybe storing operation results in WebAssembly memory.

This fundamental program will serve as a stepping stone, and the regular application of it will make it possible for you to perceive the gradual addition of complexity, which will foster a smooth learning curve. The true allure is in the process of taking something uncomplicated and observing its development into something complex and multidimensional.

Crafting WebAssembly Program

Incorporating all that we've learned so far, you will craft a WebAssembly program that will not only perform arithmetic operations but also handle data input/output, memory management, and module interactions. For this demonstration, you will lean on JavaScript for the integration, given its prevalent role in web applications.

Designing WebAssembly Module

You will create a slightly more complex version of our arithmetic program. This module will store recent results in memory and allow retrieval.

```
(module
  ;; Memory declaration
  (memory (export "memory") 1)

  ;; Store the last result at index 0
  (global $lastResult i32 (i32.const 0))

  ;; Addition
  (func (export "add") (param $x i32) (param $y i32) (result i32)
    get_local $x
    get_local $y
    i32.add
    global.set $lastResult
  )

  ;; Retrieve the last result
  (func (export "getLastResult") (result i32)
    global.get $lastResult
  )
)
```

In this module:

- We declare memory which can be accessed and manipulated from both WebAssembly and JavaScript.
- We've set up a global variable $lastResult to store the result of the last operation.
- The add function has been updated to store its result in $lastResult.

Integrating with JavaScript

We shall tie our module to a simple web interface using JavaScript.

```
async function loadWasmModule() {
  const response = await fetch('extended_arithmetic.wasm');
  const buffer = await response.arrayBuffer();
  const moduleObject = await WebAssembly.compile(buffer);
  const instance = await WebAssembly.instantiate(moduleObject);

  return instance.exports;
}

async function runWasm() {
  const wasmExports = await loadWasmModule();

  // Input from user
  const num1 = parseInt(document.getElementById("number1").value, 10);
  const num2 = parseInt(document.getElementById("number2").value, 10);

  const result = wasmExports.add(num1, num2);
  document.getElementById("output").innerText = "Addition Result: " + result;

  // Fetch and display the last result from memory
  const lastResult = wasmExports.getLastResult();
  document.getElementById("lastResult").innerText = "Last Result: " + lastResult;
}
```

```
document.getElementById("calculate").addEventListener("click", runWasm);

HTML:
<input type="number" id="number1" placeholder="Enter first number">
<input type="number" id="number2" placeholder="Enter second number">
<button id="calculate">Calculate</button>
<p id="output"></p>
<p id="lastResult"></p>
```

This HTML-JavaScript setup:

- Captures input from the user.
- Invokes the WebAssembly module's add function.
- Displays the output and also shows the last stored result.

Modules in WebAssembly, as we've learned, encapsulate related functionalities. Imagine having multiple such modules – one for arithmetic operations, another for geometric calculations, and so forth. These modules can be combined in a hierarchical fashion or run in tandem, broadening the capability of your WebAssembly-powered application. Leveraging the concept of importing and exporting functions and data, different modules can seamlessly interact, laying the foundation for modular and maintainable applications.

Deep Diving Memory Management

Memory in WebAssembly is a contiguous array of bytes, representing the linear memory. Both the WebAssembly module and its host environment (like JavaScript) can access this memory. To shed more light on this concept, we shall take a hypothetical situation where we have to deal with an extensive dataset that requires frequent manipulation. In traditional setups, passing this dataset back and forth between WebAssembly and JavaScript can create a performance bottleneck. Such a situation is far from ideal, especially when performance is a critical requirement. However, WebAssembly's memory management capabilities provide a robust solution to this challenge. By positioning the large dataset directly into WebAssembly's linear memory, we can streamline the interaction between the two. This setup allows both JavaScript and WebAssembly to work collaboratively on the same dataset without the need for redundant copying or transmission, thereby preserving both computational and temporal resources.

In the learnings we've had before, the examples showcased were relatively simple and focused on storing the last result in memory. While these examples were introductory in nature, real-world applications often demand more advanced memory management techniques. For instance, if you're building data-intensive applications like a video editor or a real-time analytics dashboard, the need for efficient memory operations becomes paramount.

One of the ways to achieve this is by making use of WebAssembly's specific memory instructions like **i32.load** and **i32.store**. These instructions allow you to directly manipulate segments of the linear memory, enabling more granular control over data. They are particularly useful in scenarios where you have to perform low-level operations, perhaps as part of an optimization strategy. But WebAssembly's memory management doesn't operate in a vacuum; it often works in tandem with JavaScript features to bring about more effective results. For instance, JavaScript provides advanced objects like **DataView** and **TypedArray**, designed to work with binary data. These objects can directly interact with WebAssembly's linear memory, allowing for a powerful and efficient way to read and write to memory sections. The **DataView** object can be used to read and write multiple number types from WebAssembly's memory in a platform-independent way. Meanwhile, **TypedArray** provides a convenient way to deal with typed arrays of integers and floating-point numbers, offering methods and properties for reading and writing data within WebAssembly memory. When used together, these JavaScript and WebAssembly features form a potent combination, providing a comprehensive toolkit for sophisticated memory management tasks.

Summary

In this chapter, we delved deep into the intricacies of WebAssembly (WASM), starting with its textual format, an intermediate representation that serves as a human-readable counterpart to its binary format. The WASM text format aids in understanding and debugging WebAssembly code, setting a clear distinction from the compact binary format tailored for machine execution. We then ventured into the realm of data types, which are foundational to any programming endeavor. In WASM, there are basic types such as integers (i32, i64) and floating-point numbers (f32, f64). These data types play a crucial role when defining functions, variables, and performing operations. Variables in WASM are declared and manipulated using local instructions. These instructions, like local.get and local.set, allow developers to store and retrieve values, making WASM efficient and expressive.

Control structures in WASM, like block, loop, and if, provide the mechanism to shape the flow of operations, enabling complex logic execution. Functions, the building blocks of modular code, in WASM are designed with reusability in mind. They accept parameters, return results, and can be called from within WASM or externally from JavaScript, ensuring a seamless interplay between the two. Memory management in WASM, represented as a linear, contiguous block of bytes, facilitates data storage and retrieval, ensuring that both WASM and its host environment have efficient access to shared data. Finally, our exploration brought us to modules – the encapsulated units of WebAssembly code. Modules promote code organization, reusability, and maintainability. They can import and export functions and variables, allowing for modular interactions within the

WASM ecosystem. We wrapped up the chapter with a hands-on approach, crafting a comprehensive WebAssembly program that harmoniously integrated all the concepts covered. This program, centered around arithmetic operations, was not just theoretical but directly interacted with a web interface, signifying the real-world applicability of WebAssembly.

Chapter 3: WebAssembly Modules and Semantics

Up to this point, we have explored the fundamental architecture of WebAssembly modules, which serve as the fundamental building blocks of any WebAssembly application. We investigated the compilation process, paying particular attention to the transformation of source code written in languages such as C, C++, and Rust into WebAssembly bytecode. We also touched on the WebAssembly Text Format (WAT), which is a representation of this bytecode that is intermediate and readable by humans. The WebAssembly runtime, which resides within the browser and offers the bytecode a secure and effective environment in which to execute, is essential to the operations described here.

As we move on to Chapter 3, we will build upon this foundation by exploring the complexities of WebAssembly module imports and exports. We are going to investigate the ways in which these modules communicate with JavaScript in order to achieve a seamless integration of functionality and performance. This chapter will also present advanced module features such as user-defined sections and the WebAssembly JavaScript Application Programming Interface (API). By doing so, we will not only learn how to optimize module interactions, but we will also learn how to tap into the full potential of WebAssembly to create applications that are both faster and more robust.

Importing and Exporting Functions

The ability to seamlessly import and export functions is one of the core strengths of WebAssembly, acting as a bridge between WASM modules and their environments, be it JavaScript or other WASM modules. This feature promotes modularity, code reusability, and interoperability. We shall dive into the mechanics of this process and explore practical demonstrations.

Import Mechanism

Import Descriptors

At its core, importing a function into a WASM module requires a descriptor. This descriptor, typically a tuple, consists of a module name and a name for the imported entity. For instance, if we wish to import a function named calculate from a module named mathLib, our descriptor would look like ("mathLib", "calculate").

Types and Imports

It's essential to ensure that the type signature of the imported function matches its usage within the WASM module. For instance, if calculate is supposed to take two 32-bit integers and return a 32-bit integer, the WebAssembly module must recognize and respect this signature.

Demonstrating Function Import

```
(module
  (import "mathLib" "calculate" (func $calc (param i32 i32) (result i32)))
  ;; Use the imported function
  (func (export "invokeCalculate")
    (param i32 i32) (result i32)
    local.get 0
    local.get 1
    call $calc
  )
)
```

In the above sample program, the function calculate is imported from mathLib. It's then wrapped in an exported function invokeCalculate which invokes the imported function.

Export Mechanism

Export Descriptors

Exporting is more straightforward. Any WebAssembly entity—function, memory, or global variable—can be tagged with an export descriptor. This descriptor essentially "marks" the entity as available for external use.

Demonstrating Function Export

```
(module
  (func (export "add") (param i32 i32) (result i32)
    local.get 0
    local.get 1
    i32.add
  )
)
```

In this snippet, we've defined a simple addition function named add. By using the (export "add") descriptor, the function becomes accessible to external modules or environments, like JavaScript.

Interaction with JavaScript

Given WebAssembly's browser-centric ecosystem, it's a common scenario to import/export functions to/from JavaScript. We shall observe this in action.

Importing from JavaScript

```
const mathLib = {
  calculate: (a, b) => a + b
};

// Assuming our previous WASM module is named `wasmModule`
const instance = new WebAssembly.Instance(wasmModule, { mathLib });
console.log(instance.exports.invokeCalculate(5, 3)); // Outputs 8
```

We provided an imported function (calculate) from JavaScript to our WebAssembly module and invoked it using the exported invokeCalculate.

Exporting to JavaScript

Once our WASM module (containing the add function) is instantiated in JavaScript, the function can be invoked directly:

```
// Assuming our WASM module is named `wasmModule`
const instance = new WebAssembly.Instance(wasmModule);
console.log(instance.exports.add(5, 3)); // Outputs 8
```

Here, the add function has been exported to JavaScript and is used just like a regular JS function.

Modules can simultaneously import and export functions, serving as intermediaries. This ability empowers developers to craft modular applications where WebAssembly modules play specific roles, each contributing to the broader functionality. In our journey through WebAssembly, mastering the mechanisms of importing and exporting is paramount. They provide the conduits through which WASM communicates, facilitating a vast range of use-cases, from mathematical computations to graphical rendering.

Table and Memory Semantics

WebAssembly encapsulates data storage and function referencing through two key concepts: memory and tables. These form the cornerstone of data access and function invocation, empowering developers to handle dynamic data and manage indirect function calls.

WebAssembly Memory

WebAssembly's memory model represents a resizable array buffer, facilitating byte-level access. Every WebAssembly module can declare its own memory, and this can be shared or imported/exported among other modules or with the embedding environment.

Memory Declaration

To declare memory within a WebAssembly module:

```
(memory $mem 1)
```

Here, $mem is a memory instance with an initial size of 1 page (64 KiB). Memory size is always measured in pages.

Memory Access

To read and write values to memory, WebAssembly provides a set of load and store instructions.

Example, loading and storing a 32-bit integer:

```
;; Store 42 at offset 0
i32.const 42
i32.const 0
i32.store

;; Load integer from offset 0
i32.const 0
i32.load
```

Resizing Memory

WebAssembly memory can be resized using the grow instruction. For instance, to grow memory by one page:

```
i32.const 1
memory.grow
```

WebAssembly Tables

Tables in WebAssembly are resizable typed arrays of references, not bytes. While memory serves to store raw data, tables are primarily used to store function references for indirect function calls.

Table Declaration

To declare a table within a WebAssembly module:

```
(table $tbl 1 funcref)
```

Here, $tbl is a table with an initial size of 1, holding function references (funcref).

Accessing and Modifying Tables

Tables can be accessed and modified using the get and set instructions.

Example, setting and getting from a table:

```
;; Set the first entry to a function $func
i32.const 0
func.ref $func
table.set $tbl

;; Get the function reference from the first entry
i32.const 0
table.get $tbl
```

Resizing Tables

Similar to memory, tables can be resized using the grow instruction:

```
i32.const 1
table.grow $tbl
```

Practical Exploration of Memory and Table Semantics

Memory in Action

Consider the use case of a simple string manipulation program in WebAssembly. This program will store two strings in memory, compute their lengths, and append them.

```
(module
  ;; Memory declaration
  (memory $mem 1)
  (data (i32.const 0) "Hello")
  (data (i32.const 5) " World")
  ;; Function to append strings
  (func $appendStrings
    ;; Logic to append strings goes here
    ;; This involves loading characters from memory
    ;; and storing the result back in memory.
  )
  (export "invoke" (func $appendStrings))
)
```

This simple module declares a memory, places two strings in it, and provides a function to append them.

Table Semantics

Consider a module that provides different mathematical operations like addition, subtraction, multiplication, and division. A table can be used to store references to these functions, allowing the calling program to choose an operation based on a provided index.

```
(module
  ;; Table declaration
  (table $tbl 4 funcref)
  (elem (i32.const 0) $add $sub $mul $div)
  ;; Functions
```

```
  (func $add (param i32 i32) (result i32) ...)
  (func $sub (param i32 i32) (result i32) ...)
  (func $mul (param i32 i32) (result i32) ...)
  (func $div (param i32 i32) (result i32) ...)
  ;; Function to execute an operation based on an index
  (func $executeOp (param i32 i32 i32) (result i32)
    (param $idx i32) ;; index of the operation in the table
    ;; Logic to perform the operation using table.get
  )
  (export "invokeOp" (func $executeOp))
)
```

In this module, a table holds references to four mathematical functions. The exported function $executeOp performs a selected operation based on the provided index.

Event-Driven Programming in WebAssembly

The idea of event-driven programming has its origins deep within the field of computer science and is primarily concerned with the design and architecture of software programs. It is predicated on the notion that particular components of a program are put into action in reaction to particular occurrences, such as actions performed by the user, outputs from sensors, or messages sent by other programs. The use of event-driven programming is common in user interfaces, real-time systems, and a wide variety of other applications. It is an essential component of interactive systems.

WebAssembly's Execution Model and Events

WebAssembly (WASM) predominantly came into the scene as a compilation target for web applications. Given the inherently event-driven nature of web applications—with user interactions, AJAX requests, and other browser events—it's natural to ask: How does WebAssembly fit into the event-driven paradigm?

WebAssembly has been designed to run code in a web environment, and by extension, it inherently supports an event-driven model. However, it's worth noting that WebAssembly itself does not define any event-handling operations in its core specification. Instead, it relies on its host environment (typically the browser) to handle events and invoke WebAssembly functions in response.

Interactions with JavaScript

Given that WebAssembly does not have built-in event listeners or handlers, its event-driven capabilities are facilitated by its seamless interoperability with JavaScript. Events are captured by JavaScript, which then can call WebAssembly exported functions. This collaboration harnesses the power of WebAssembly's performance and JavaScript's vast ecosystem. For instance, a button click in a web page can trigger a JavaScript event listener, which in turn invokes a WebAssembly function to execute computationally intensive operations.

WebAssembly's execution within the browser context integrates with the browser's event loop. When a WebAssembly module is instantiated, it does not block the main thread, ensuring that the responsiveness of the user interface is maintained. This non-blocking behavior is crucial for the efficient functioning of event-driven web applications.

Advantages of Event-Driven WebAssembly

Improved Responsiveness

One of the primary advantages of incorporating WebAssembly into event-driven architecture is the noticeable improvement in application responsiveness. By delegating computationally heavy tasks to WebAssembly while retaining event handling in JavaScript, we achieve an optimized, non-blocking user experience. This balanced division of labor between JavaScript and WebAssembly ensures that the application remains highly interactive, responsive, and efficient, even during complex data processing or calculations.

Concurrency

The importance of concurrency in modern web applications cannot be overstated, and WebAssembly has made significant strides in this department with the introduction of WebAssembly threads. These threads provide the ability to manage multiple tasks in parallel, thereby paving the way for even more responsive and robust event-driven applications. Concurrency in WebAssembly enables different tasks to be handled concurrently, without causing lags or jitters in the user interface, making for a smoother overall user experience.

Portability

Another hallmark of WebAssembly is its platform-agnostic nature, which makes it an ideal choice for event-driven architectures. Applications designed using WebAssembly can be effortlessly ported across various platforms, provided they support a WebAssembly-compatible browser. This level of portability ensures that event-driven applications built on WebAssembly can potentially cater to a wide range of devices and operating systems without requiring separate builds or extensive modifications.

Enhanced Performance

Last but not least, WebAssembly provides a significant boost in the performance arena, especially useful for event-driven applications requiring heavy computations. Because of its closer-to-metal execution capabilities, WebAssembly can perform resource-intensive tasks more efficiently than JavaScript. This advantage becomes particularly valuable in scenarios where event handlers are called upon to perform computationally demanding operations. WebAssembly can step in and execute these tasks swiftly, ensuring that the application maintains its speed and responsiveness. As the specification evolves and new capabilities get added, the synergy between WebAssembly and event-driven paradigms will only grow stronger

Building Event-Driven Microservices

The modern landscape of software design has evolved to favor microservices, which are independent, single-purpose services that can operate and scale autonomously. Given WebAssembly's capabilities and izts prowess in the realm of event-driven programming, it offers a compelling platform for building efficient, lightweight, and cross-platform microservices. In this segment, we will explore how to build an event-driven microservice using WebAssembly.

Considering our prior learnings, we shall build upon the real-time gaming scenario. Imagine we're developing a multiplayer online game where players can trade in-game items. You will create an event-driven microservice that listens for trade requests and processes them, all built atop WebAssembly.

Setting up Environment

Firstly, to develop WebAssembly modules, we would ideally use languages like Rust, C, or C++. For our purpose, you will continue using Rust as used in the past.

Installing Rust and wasm-pack

Begin by installing Rust. Following that, get wasm-pack, a tool for assembling and packaging Rust-generated WebAssembly.

```
curl --proto '=https' --tlsv1.2 -sSf https://sh.rustup.rs/ | sh
cargo install wasm-pack
```

Crafting WebAssembly Module

Next, create a new Rust project:

```
cargo new wasm_trade_service
```

Within this, define the logic for our trading system:

```
// src/lib.rs

extern crate wasm_bindgen;
use wasm_bindgen::prelude::*;

#[wasm_bindgen]
pub struct TradeService;

#[wasm_bindgen]
impl TradeService {
  #[wasm_bindgen(constructor)]
  pub fn new() -> TradeService {
    TradeService {}
  }

  pub fn process_trade(&self, trade_data: &str) -> String {
    // ... processing logic here ...
    format!("Processed trade: {}", trade_data)
  }
}
```

Build the module with:

```
wasm-pack build --target web
```

Event-driven Logic with JavaScript

Since WASM itself doesn't provide event-driven primitives, JavaScript will capture the events, invoking our WASM module's functions in response. We shall assume an event source emits an event when a player initiates a trade. Following is a hypothetical implementation using Node.js with an EventEmitter:

```
const events = require('events');
const wasm = require('./path_to_generated_wasm.js');  // adjust the path accordingly
```

```
const tradeEmitter = new events.EventEmitter();

wasm.init('./path_to_generated_wasm_bg.wasm').then(() => {
  const tradeService = wasm.TradeService.new();

  tradeEmitter.on('newTrade', (tradeData) => {
    const result = tradeService.process_trade(tradeData);
    console.log(result);
  });
});

// Simulating a trade event
tradeEmitter.emit('newTrade', 'Trade between Player A and Player B');
```

Deploying Microservice

Once our WebAssembly microservice is ready, it's time for deployment. Depending on your ecosystem, this might involve deploying to a cloud provider or integrating it within a containerized environment using tools like Docker. For WebAssembly modules, solutions like Wasmer can run WASM outside the browser, providing an ideal platform for microservices. Given the event-driven nature, it's easy to scale our WebAssembly microservice. Each instance of the microservice can listen to trade events independently, ensuring high availability and fault tolerance. In practice, you'd have your event source (like a message queue or event grid) distribute trade events among various instances of your microservice. This way, even if player trading activity spikes suddenly, our architecture can accommodate without a hitch.

Through this exploration, we've seen how WebAssembly can be a potent tool in the realm of event-driven microservices.

WebAssembly Linear Memory

One of the most fundamental and powerful features of WebAssembly is its linear memory model. It's essential for understanding how data moves between your WASM modules and their host environments, as well as how the WASM module manages its own internal state.

Understanding Linear Memory

WebAssembly's memory model is both simple and flexible, operating as a contiguous, resizable array of bytes known as linear memory. This memory serves as the primary mechanism by which data is stored and manipulated within a WASM module.

- Contiguous Array of Bytes: The most straightforward way to think of linear memory is as a vast array, where each index points to a byte of memory. These bytes can represent anything: integers, floats, strings, etc.

- Isolation and Security: This memory is isolated from the host environment, meaning it can't directly access or be accessed by external memory, ensuring robust security.

- Resizable: While WebAssembly memory starts with an initial size, it can be expanded if needed, though there is an upper limit defined by the platform.

Whenever you compile a program into WASM, variables, data structures, and other elements are mapped into this linear memory. This mapping allows for operations on this data within the module.

Accessing and Manipulating Linear Memory

Linear memory can be accessed and manipulated through specific operations:

- load: Read data from memory.

- store: Write data to memory.

For instance, if you had an integer stored at position 0 in memory, you might use a load operation to retrieve it or a store operation to change its value.

Working with Linear Memory

We shall delve into a hands-on example to illustrate how linear memory works, building on our previous learnings about a multiplayer online game. Suppose we want to store player scores in WebAssembly memory.

Setting up Environment

Firstly, using Rust, create a new WASM project:

```
cargo new wasm_scores
```

Defining Memory Structure

In the lib.rs file:

```
extern crate wasm_bindgen;
use wasm_bindgen::prelude::*;
use wasm_bindgen::memory;

#[wasm_bindgen]
pub struct PlayerScore {
    player_id: u32,
    score: u32,
}

#[wasm_bindgen]
pub fn store_player_score(player_id: u32, score: u32) {
    let memory = memory::Memory::new(1);  // Create 1 page of memory (64KiB)
    let buffer = memory.view::<u8>();

    buffer[player_id as usize * 8].set(player_id as u8); // Store player ID
    buffer[player_id as usize * 8 + 4].set(score as u8); // Store player score
}

#[wasm_bindgen]
pub fn retrieve_player_score(player_id: u32) -> PlayerScore {
    let memory = memory::Memory::new(1);
    let buffer = memory.view::<u8>();

    let pid = buffer[player_id as usize * 8].get();
    let score = buffer[player_id as usize * 8 + 4].get();

    PlayerScore {
        player_id: pid as u32,
```

```
        score: score as u32,
    }
}
```

This Rust code sets up memory operations to store and retrieve player scores. The store_player_score function receives a player's ID and score, then stores these in linear memory. The retrieve_player_score function fetches this data back from memory.

```
const wasm = require('./path_to_generated_wasm.js');


wasm.init().then(() => {
    wasm.store_player_score(1, 5000);
    const playerScore = wasm.retrieve_player_score(1);
    console.log(`Player ID: ${playerScore.player_id}, Score: ${playerScore.score}`);
});
```

With the WASM module compiled, you can then interact with the linear memory in JavaScript.

Structuring Large-Sized WASM Apps

As applications grow in complexity, proper structuring becomes crucial to ensure maintainability, scalability, and comprehensibility. This applies equally to WebAssembly projects. Below are tactics and strategies to effectively structure and manage large WASM applications.

Modularize Codebase

Functionality-based Modules

Divide your code into modules based on distinct functionalities. For instance, in our multiplayer game scenario, separate modules for player management, in-game transactions, score management, etc., could be created.

```
// player.rs
pub struct Player { /*...*/ }
impl Player { /*...*/ }


// transactions.rs
pub struct Transaction { /*...*/ }
```

```
impl Transaction { /*...*/ }
```

Shared Utilities

Common functionalities and utilities, such as error handling or mathematical operations, should reside in shared modules, preventing code repetition. WASI (WebAssembly System Interface) and WebAssembly Interface Types can be instrumental for large projects. Interface Types allow for richer interaction between WASM modules and their host environment, reducing the need for boilerplate and facilitating more direct data interchange.

Prioritize Component Reusability

Aim to build components that can be reused across different parts of the application or even in other projects.

Generic Components

If you find that certain components (like a leaderboard manager) could be reused with minor variations, consider making them generic.

```
pub struct Manager<T> {
    items: Vec<T>,
    // ...
}
```

Well-Defined Interfaces

Ensure each module has a clear, well-defined interface. This not only makes modules reusable but also allows for easier testing and validation.

Interoperability Considerations

Large applications often require integrating with numerous other systems or services.

JavaScript Interactions

Use tools like wasm-bindgen to handle interaction between WASM and JavaScript smoothly. Ensure a clean interface between the two, keeping them as decoupled as possible.

Foreign Function Interface (FFI)

If you're integrating with C or C++ libraries, use Rust's FFI capabilities to interact with these libraries seamlessly.

Effective State Management

State management becomes critical as applications scale. Consider strategies and patterns like:

Singleton Patterns

For components that should be instantiated just once, such as a game manager or configuration loader.

Immutable Data Structures

Consider leveraging Rust's ownership model to create immutable data structures, ensuring safer concurrent operations.

Error Handling and Logging

A comprehensive error handling and logging mechanism is indispensable for spotting and troubleshooting issues.

Custom Error Types

Define custom error types using Rust's enum and Result types. This offers clarity on what kinds of errors different parts of the application might encounter.

```
enum GameError {
    PlayerNotFound,
    InvalidTransaction,
    // ...
}
```

Logging

Implement a logging mechanism to record crucial application events. Consider integrating with external logging solutions or platforms if the application is deployed in a distributed environment.

Testing and Validation

Ensure that each module or component is accompanied by thorough unit tests. Integration tests, which validate the interactions between modules, become even more vital in larger applications.

Mocking and Stubs

Use mocking and stubs to simulate external services or components, ensuring tests are isolated and reproducible.

Performance Testing
Given that one of WebAssembly's attractions is its performance, periodically run performance benchmarks, especially as new features or changes are introduced.

Security and Optimization

As with any application, especially large ones:

- Optimization: Regularly profile your application, identifying bottlenecks and areas of potential optimization.

- Security Audits: Large applications can be vulnerable to security lapses. Regularly conduct security audits and be aware of best practices to ensure your application's integrity.

While large WebAssembly applications present their challenges, a structured approach combined with the strategies above can help manage complexity. Prioritize modularity, reusability, robust tooling, and continuous learning to navigate the intricacies of large-scale WebAssembly development effectively.

Error Handling in WebAssembly

Error handling is one of the key aspects of any application, ensuring that unexpected scenarios or issues are dealt with gracefully without causing disruptions. WebAssembly, being a relatively low-level runtime, initially didn't include built-in mechanisms for exceptions. However, as the ecosystem has grown, various techniques have been developed to manage errors, especially when WebAssembly interacts with languages that do support exceptions, like Rust or C++.

In traditional programming environments, errors can be managed using exceptions, status returns, or callbacks. WebAssembly's core doesn't yet natively support exceptions like high-level languages, but the host environment (often JavaScript) does. This dichotomy poses unique challenges and opportunities.

Return Codes

One of the most straightforward methods to handle errors in WebAssembly is by returning status codes from functions. This is akin to many C libraries where functions return specific codes indicating success or different types of failures.

For example, consider a WebAssembly function designed to handle player registration in our multiplayer game scenario:

```
pub fn register_player(name: &str) -> i32 {
    if name.is_empty() {
        return -1; // Error code for an empty name.
    }
    // ... rest of the registration logic.
    return 0; // Success.
}
```

In this rudimentary example, -1 indicates an error while 0 indicates success.
1

Multiple Return Values

Languages like Rust allow functions to return multiple values, which can be used to return both a result and an error status. This can be particularly useful when translating Rust's Result type to WebAssembly.

```
pub fn calculate_score(player_id: i32) -> (i32, i32) {
    if player_not_found(player_id) {
        return (-1, 404); // -1 as error, 404 as Player Not Found.
    }
    let score = compute_score(player_id);
    return (score, 0); // Return score and a success status.
}
```

Here, the first value is the actual result, and the second value is the status code.

Using Linear Memory

Another approach involves using WebAssembly's linear memory to store error messages or details. When a function encounters an error, it can write the error details into memory, which the caller can then read and interpret.

Consider a function that tries to retrieve player details:

```
enum PlayerError {
    NotFound,
    DatabaseError,
```

```
}

pub fn get_player_details(player_id: i32) -> Result<Player, PlayerError> {
    if database_connection_failed() {
        return Err(PlayerError::DatabaseError);
    } else if player_not_found(player_id) {
        return Err(PlayerError::NotFound);
    }
    // Fetch and return player details.
    let player = fetch_player_from_db(player_id);
    Ok(player)
}
```

In this approach, the Result type encapsulates either the actual result or the error. The specific nature of the error is described by the custom PlayerError enum.

Proposed Exception Handling for WebAssembly

The WebAssembly community is working on introducing native exception handling. This will allow languages with built-in exception mechanisms, like C++ or Rust, to compile to WebAssembly more effectively. This proposal would introduce constructs to throw and catch exceptions directly in the WebAssembly code. Although it's still in the proposal stage, it promises to bring richer error handling capabilities to WebAssembly.

Sample Program: Error Handling in Multiplayer Game

We shall explore error handling using the multiplayer game example previously learned. Imagine we want to create a function that adds a player to a game session:

```
enum GameError {
    PlayerLimitReached,
    InvalidPlayerData,
    SessionNotFound,
}

pub fn add_player_to_session(session_id: i32, player: Player) -> Result<(), GameError>
{
    // Check if session exists
```

```
    if !session_exists(session_id) {
        return Err(GameError::SessionNotFound);
    }

    // Validate player data
    if !player.is_valid() {
        return Err(GameError::InvalidPlayerData);
    }

    // Check if session has room for more players
    if session_is_full(session_id) {
        return Err(GameError::PlayerLimitReached);
    }

    // Logic to add player to the session
    // ...

    // If everything went fine, return Ok
    Ok(())
}
```

In the host environment (e.g., JavaScript), when calling this WebAssembly function, you'd check the result and handle the error accordingly:

```
const result = wasmInstance.exports.add_player_to_session(sessionId, player);
if (result instanceof GameError) {
    switch(result) {
        case GameError.SessionNotFound:
            console.error("Session not found!");
            break;
        case GameError.InvalidPlayerData:
            console.error("Player data is invalid!");
            break;
        case GameError.PlayerLimitReached:
            console.error("Session is full!");
```

```
        break;
    }
}
```

Through this example, we've showcased how Rust's Result type can be leveraged for expressive error handling in WebAssembly and how those errors can be interpreted and managed in the host environment.

WebAssembly System Interface (WASI)

WebAssembly, in its early stages, was primarily a sandboxed runtime focused on the web. This meant that WebAssembly modules couldn't directly access system resources like the file system, networking, or even direct hardware access. While this sandboxing brought a high degree of security, it also limited WebAssembly's capabilities outside of a browser context. This is where the WebAssembly System Interface (WASI) enters the scene.

WASI is designed to expand the potential of WebAssembly beyond the browser. It offers a standardized interface for WebAssembly modules to access system resources, thereby enabling developers to build standalone WebAssembly applications that can run in various environments, be it the cloud, on personal computers, or even embedded devices.

Philosophy and Design Principles

One of the cornerstone philosophies of WASI (WebAssembly System Interface) is portability. The aim here is to reinforce WebAssembly's core principle of "Write Once, Run Anywhere." To achieve this, WASI provides a set of well-defined APIs meticulously designed for cross-platform compatibility. The vision is that a WebAssembly module developed with WASI in mind should be capable of running on a variety of platforms with minimal or no modifications. This cross-platform compatibility not only enhances developer experience but also expands the reach of WebAssembly modules to diverse systems and environments.

Another central pillar in WASI's design philosophy is security, specifically aligning with WebAssembly's overarching principle of least authority. In a practical sense, this means that a WASI module starts with zero permissions by default. Access to various system resources or capabilities must be explicitly granted, usually during the instantiation process. This capability-based security model minimizes risks associated with running untrusted or third-party modules. By requiring explicit permission grants, WASI ensures that a module can only perform actions that it has been specifically allowed to, thereby reducing the surface area for potential security threats.

WASI is not conceptualized as a single, all-encompassing API. Instead, it adopts a modular approach to system interfaces, dividing them into specific functional blocks or capabilities. Each module focuses on a particular type of system resource or capability, such as file I/O or networking. This modular construction allows host systems flexibility in implementation; they can choose to support only the WASI modules that are relevant to their use case. This tailored approach enables streamlined adoption and allows host systems to scale their capabilities progressively, making the integration of new functionalities more manageable and efficient.

Capabilities and Functionalities

In the era prior to the WebAssembly System Interface (WASI), attaining direct access to a file system was a considerable hurdle for WebAssembly modules. However, WASI has fundamentally altered this dynamic. Now, WebAssembly modules are equipped with the capability to not only read from and write to files but also to inspect file metadata, such as size and modification date. They can even manage directory structures, including creating, deleting, and navigating through directories, given that they possess the requisite permissions for these actions.

Before WASI, network interactions were something of a sticking point for WebAssembly. WASI has revolutionized this by introducing standardized Application Programming Interfaces (APIs) that WebAssembly modules can utilize. These APIs empower modules to make HTTP or TCP network requests, thereby facilitating their communication with other services or databases over the internet. This has expanded the horizons for WebAssembly modules, enabling a wide range of networked applications.

On the surface, the capability to generate random numbers might appear inconsequential. However, in reality, randomness plays a pivotal role in various applications, especially those that hinge on cryptographic operations for secure data transfer or authentication. WASI alleviates this challenge by providing a standardized method for WebAssembly modules to acquire random data, enhancing security and functionality.

Knowing the current time is more than just a convenience; it's a necessity for many applications. Whether it's timestamping events for audit trails, scheduling tasks, or calculating durations for performance metrics, time is often of the essence. WASI provides functions that allow WebAssembly modules to accurately retrieve the current time, thereby offering the ability to implement a wide array of time-sensitive operations.

Configuration settings are often supplied through environment variables, especially in containerized or cloud-native applications. Before WASI, WebAssembly modules had limited ways to interact with these variables. Now, WASI enables WebAssembly modules to access, read, and even modify environment variables. This capability can be particularly instrumental for dynamically configuring modules based on the settings of the environment in which they are deployed, thereby offering greater adaptability and flexibility.

WASI's emergence holds significant implications for the broader software landscape. A few of these are:

- Portability: With WASI, applications can be compiled once and run in various environments without modification. This offers immense potential for application distribution and deployment.

- Edge Computing: As WebAssembly can run in lightweight, isolated environments, combined with WASI's system access capabilities, there's significant potential for WebAssembly in edge computing scenarios. Applications can be run closer to the data source, be it IoT devices or edge servers.

- Containerization and Microservices: WASI can streamline containerized applications by providing lightweight, fast-starting, and secure modules, ideal for microservices architectures.

- Game Development: WASI allows game developers to write game logic that runs both in the browser (for web-based games) and natively (for desktop or mobile games). This could lead to better cross-platform game engines and tools.

Recall our multiplayer game example. With WASI, developers can write game logic in languages like Rust or C++, compile it to a WebAssembly module with WASI support, and then run that module both on game servers and in the browser.

On the server-side, the WebAssembly module could manage game sessions, handle player data, and even run AI logic, all while interacting with system resources like the file system or databases through WASI. The same module, when loaded in a web browser, can run the game client, accessing local resources if needed, and communicating with the server. This seamless portability ensures that the game logic remains consistent across platforms while reducing development overheads.

WebAssembly Threads

WebAssembly's initial design was single-threaded, with concurrency managed outside the WebAssembly module. However, as applications become more complex and demand better performance, concurrency becomes essential. WebAssembly Threads is a proposal that extends WebAssembly's capabilities, allowing for the creation and manipulation of threads within a WebAssembly context.

Understanding Threads

Threads, in the broader computing context, are the smallest sequences of programmed instructions that can be managed independently by a scheduler. They allow for parallel execution of tasks, making optimal use of multicore processors. Threads share the same memory space, which allows them to communicate and coordinate easily, but it also necessitates synchronization mechanisms to prevent conflicts.

Why Threads in WebAssembly?

The foremost advantage of employing multithreading in WebAssembly applications is the significant boost in performance. Multithreaded applications can take full advantage of multiple CPU cores, operating them concurrently. This leads to a noticeable increase in the speed of execution and application responsiveness, which is particularly beneficial for compute-intensive tasks and real-time applications.

In today's digital age, concurrency is not just a fancy feature but a necessity. Real-world applications often require multiple operations to execute simultaneously. Imagine a gaming application where you need to load the game level, play background music, monitor player input, and perhaps even stream content—all at the same time. Multithreading enables such high levels of concurrency, making applications more robust and user-friendly.

Efficient use of available computational resources is critical for any application's performance and usability. Distributing computational work across multiple threads allows for better resource optimization. It enables applications to manage multiple tasks more effectively, reducing idle time and improving overall throughput.

Core Features of WebAssembly Threads

- Shared Memory: One of the key features that WebAssembly Threads introduce is shared memory capabilities via the SharedArrayBuffer object. This opens up the possibility for multiple WebAssembly threads, and even JavaScript when operating in a browser context, to read from and write to the same memory space concurrently. This shared memory model facilitates more complex, efficient, and faster data manipulations and computations.

- Atomic Operations: Multithreading often introduces the complexity of data races, where multiple threads attempt to read or write to shared data simultaneously. To counter this, WebAssembly Threads include a range of atomic operations. These atomic operations ensure that specific memory operations are executed in a manner that they are completed without being interrupted, thereby maintaining data integrity and consistency.

- Mutexes and Synchronization: In addition to low-level atomic operations, WebAssembly Threads also provide higher-level synchronization primitives like mutexes. These mutexes, or mutual exclusion constructs, enable more advanced coordination between threads. They ensure that only one thread can access a particular piece of code or data at any given time, thereby preventing race conditions and making it easier to write thread-safe code.

Working with WebAssembly Threads

We shall illustrate threads in WebAssembly through an example involving our recurring theme: a multiplayer game. Imagine you want to load game assets while also rendering the game world.

Setting up Shared Memory

First, you'd declare a SharedArrayBuffer to serve as the shared memory space:

```
const sharedMemory = new SharedArrayBuffer(1024 * 1024); // 1MB buffer
```

Creating WebAssembly Instance

When instantiating your WebAssembly module, you'd pass the shared memory to both the main game logic and the asset-loading module:

```
WebAssembly.instantiate(gameWasmModule, {
  env: {
    memory: sharedMemory
  }
});

WebAssembly.instantiate(assetsWasmModule, {
  env: {
    memory: sharedMemory
  }
});
```

Performing Atomic Operations

Suppose you want to ensure that when a specific game asset is accessed by one thread, no other thread modifies it. You'd use atomic operations:

```
webassembly
(i32.atomic.load offset=0 (get_local $ptr))
```

This WebAssembly instruction atomically loads a 32-bit integer from the shared memory.

Synchronization with Mutexes

For tasks that involve multiple steps or aren't easily divided into atomic operations, you can use mutexes. While WebAssembly doesn't provide mutexes directly, they can be built using the lower-level primitives that WebAssembly offers, like atomic operations.

Considerations When Using WebAssembly Threads:

- Data Races: Just because you can access shared memory concurrently doesn't mean you always should. Care must be taken to ensure that threads don't overwrite each other's changes unexpectedly.

- Deadlocks: As with all multithreading contexts, there's a risk of deadlocks when two or more threads wait indefinitely for resources the other holds.

- Browser Support: As of my last update, WebAssembly Threads is supported in several major browsers, but it's essential to check compatibility and perhaps provide fallbacks for unsupported environments.

Let us consider an expanded scenario of the previously demonstrated multiplayer game. As players traverse the game world, new areas and assets need to be loaded. Using WebAssembly threads, the game can continue rendering the current scene and handling player interactions while a separate thread loads upcoming assets. This way, when a player reaches a new area, there's no lag or loading screen—the assets are preloaded and ready to be rendered. Meanwhile, the main game thread can offload some tasks, like AI computations or physics simulations, to secondary threads, ensuring smooth gameplay even in complex scenarios.

By using threads, the game becomes more responsive, provides a better user experience, and can handle more extensive computations without noticeable performance drops. WebAssembly Threads opens the door to high-performance, concurrent web applications. For developers coming from a systems programming background, this offers a familiar paradigm to optimize applications.

Packaging and Reusing Modules

When code is modularized, it becomes more maintainable and reusable across projects. As with many software paradigms, the idea is to write once and use in many places. We shall delve into the practice of packaging and reusing these modules with the continuation of our game example.

Need for Reusability

Our multiplayer game example has been growing in complexity. Imagine we've developed various components, such as:

- Asset Loading: A module dedicated to preloading graphics, sound effects, and other game resources.
- Physics Engine: Handling collision detection, player movement, and game-world interactions.
- AI Logic: Managing non-player characters, their decisions, and behaviors.
- If these components are modularized correctly in WebAssembly, they can be reused in other games or even different applications.

Creating Reusable WebAssembly Module

For the sake of simplicity, we shall focus on the AI Logic module. This module contains logic for NPCs (Non-Player Characters) to make decisions. We believe this logic might be useful for other games, so we aim to package it for reuse.

Ensure that the AI Logic module is decoupled from the rest of the game. It should interact with the game world through well-defined interfaces. Inputs could be current player positions, nearby obstacles, etc., and outputs might be the next action an NPC should take.

WebAssembly Code (Simplified) for AI Logic

```
(module
  ;; External function to get player's position
  (import "game" "get_player_position" (func $get_player_position (result i32 i32)))
```

```
  ;; Function to determine NPC action based on player's position
  (func $decide_npc_action (export "decide_action")
    ;; Logic here to determine action based on player position
  )
)
```

Compile to WebAssembly Binary

Once written, you'd compile your AI Logic into a .wasm binary using a compiler compatible with your source language (e.g., Emscripten for C/C++).

Package with Associated Files

If your WebAssembly module requires other resources – perhaps some data files or configuration – these should be packaged together.

Consider a directory structure:

```lua
ai-logic/
|-- ai-logic.wasm
|-- config.json
```

Reusing the WebAssembly Module

When you decide to start a new game project or any application where the AI Logic could be applied, you won't have to start from scratch.

Importing the Module

In your new project, you'd import and instantiate the AI Logic module:

```
const aiLogicBytes = fetch('path_to_ai-logic/ai-logic.wasm').then(response => response.arrayBuffer());
const aiLogicModule = await WebAssembly.instantiate(aiLogicBytes);
```

Integration

Now, integrate it with the new game. Given our module needs to know the player's position, you'd link the get_player_position function from your new game to the AI Logic module:

```
const aiLogicInstance = await WebAssembly.instantiate(aiLogicBytes, {
```

```
  game: {
    get_player_position: function() {
      // Return player's position from the new game
    }
  }
});
```

Refining Based on Feedback

As you use the AI Logic module across more games, you'll get feedback. Maybe there's a particular behavior that doesn't fit every game's context, or perhaps there are performance tweaks needed for a specific platform. This feedback loop can lead to the iterative refinement of your reusable modules, benefiting all projects that incorporate them.

Given our multiplayer game's evolving complexities, the ability to segment, package, and reuse components becomes a massive advantage. Maybe the AI Logic developed for this game finds its way into a completely different genre of game. Or the physics engine becomes the foundation for a simulation tool. As developers work on future projects, they'll find the process of integrating these pre-made, efficient, and tested WebAssembly modules to be a significant productivity boost.

Summary

In this chapter, we began an in-depth exploration of more advanced aspects of WebAssembly by reviewing modules once more as our first topic of learnings. In WASM, the most fundamental unit of binary code is a module. They contain all of the necessary functionalities, ranging from the declaration of functions that are importable or exportable to the housing of the primary application logic. The architecture encourages the use of modular application structures, which improves both the maintainability and the reusability of the architecture across different projects.

In addition, we learned the intricate details of importing and exporting functions, which is an essential component for achieving interoperability between JavaScript and WebAssembly. It is absolutely necessary to have a solid understanding of the interaction between the WebAssembly module and the JavaScript environment in order to make effective use of WASM within web applications. Developers are able to integrate WASM into their applications in a seamless manner by declaring particular functions to be either imports or exports. This enables the sharing of tasks between JavaScript and WASM. This practice ensures that each can make the most of its strengths, with WASM managing computational tasks and JavaScript managing the DOM and other web APIs. This practice ensures that each can capitalize on its strengths.

In addition, we investigated table and memory semantics, focusing on the roles that these concepts play in the management of the state and data contained within WebAssembly applications. Tables make it possible to store references to functions, which opens the door to dynamic calls and makes it easier to build more complicated application structures. Memory, on the other hand, operates as a resizable array that stores the linear memory that is accessed by the WASM module. This memory can be expanded as needed. Having a firm grasp on these ideas is absolutely necessary in order to ensure effective data management and interaction between WASM and the outside world.

The last part of the chapter focused on event-driven programming in WebAssembly and highlighted its potential use in the construction of responsive applications. We investigated how WASM can be incorporated into event-driven architectures such as microservices, which enables quick, efficient, and scalable responses to user inputs or events generated by the system. This, in conjunction with the information provided on how to handle errors, WASI, WASM threads, and application structuring, makes available to developers a comprehensive toolkit for the creation of high-performance web applications utilizing WebAssembly.

CHAPTER 4: BRIDGING WEBASSEMBLY WITH HIGH-LEVEL LANGUAGES

Compiling, Porting, and Interoperability

WebAssembly (WASM) has undoubtedly revolutionized web performance, but its true potential lies in its ability to interact and collaborate with other languages. This chapter aims to shed light on the tools, techniques, and practices to seamlessly integrate WASM with a range of popular programming languages.

Emscripten

First, meet Emscripten, often heralded as the gateway to WebAssembly for a plethora of languages. Emscripten is a toolchain that compiles C and C++ (among others) into WASM. It allows developers to run high-performance C/C++ on the web at near-native speeds. Beyond just the compiler, Emscripten offers a runtime that simulates a traditional system environment, meaning most C/C++ libraries can run without any modifications.

While Emscripten primarily focuses on C and C++, the horizon of WebAssembly is broadening with efforts to bring in other languages. Rust, for example, has a dedicated WASM target, allowing developers to compile Rust programs into WebAssembly directly. Similarly, AssemblyScript offers a TypeScript-like experience for those looking to write in a language they're familiar with, yet still, compile to WASM. This expanding ecosystem indicates a future where a multitude of languages can be compiled down to WebAssembly.

WABi Toolkit and Multi-Language Porting

Another exciting development is the WebAssembly Binary Interface (WABi) toolkit. WABi allows for easier interfacing of WASM modules, especially when they're compiled from different languages. This toolkit standardizes the way WASM modules interact, enabling more uniformity and predictability, irrespective of the source language.

Java and Python, two heavyweight languages in the programming world, are not far behind in the WASM race. For Java, tools like TeaVM allow Java bytecode to be converted into WebAssembly. This doesn't mean one can run full-fledged Java applications on WASM, but core logic can certainly be ported. Python, on the other hand, has efforts like Pyodide, which compiles the Python interpreter to WASM, enabling Python to run in the browser.

WASM Bindings and Interoperability

Bindings in WebAssembly are the bridges that allow WASM to communicate effectively with other languages, especially JavaScript. Tools like wasm-bindgen for Rust simplify the process of creating these bridges, making it easier to pass complex types, like strings or classes, between Rust and JavaScript. These bindings ensure that the interaction between WASM and its host environment is as seamless and efficient as possible.

Interoperability is the cornerstone of WebAssembly's value proposition. However, to ensure smooth operations, developers need to adhere to certain best practices. One primary consideration is understanding and respecting the strengths of each language. Instead of replacing JavaScript entirely, WASM should be seen as a complementary tool, handling tasks it's best suited for. Moreover, when porting existing applications, it's essential to understand the limitations of WASM and the performance implications. Sometimes, a hybrid approach, where core computational logic is handled by WASM while IO or DOM manipulations remain in the original language, proves to be the most efficient.

In subsequent sections, you will delve deeper into each of these areas, ensuring a comprehensive understanding of integrating WebAssembly with various programming languages, ensuring optimized performance and seamless user experience.

Exploring Emscripten

Discussing WebAssembly without giving due credit to Emscripten would be an oversight. This comprehensive toolchain has played an incredibly important role in bridging the gap between traditional software development paradigms and the revolutionary capabilities offered by WebAssembly. It serves as a catalyst in the transition of legacy code to web-compatible formats, thereby expanding the boundaries of what is possible in web development.

Emscripten's Features

Emscripten is not just another toolchain; it's a Swiss Army knife for developers looking to convert C, C++, and other statically-typed languages into a format that's readily compatible with WebAssembly. At its core, it started off as an LLVM-to-JavaScript compiler, capitalizing on the capabilities of LLVM to convert source code into high-quality JavaScript. However, with the advent and growing popularity of WebAssembly, Emscripten has broadened its horizon. It now focuses on creating WASM binaries but continues to generate the indispensable JavaScript "glue" code that interfaces seamlessly with web platforms.

Underlying Mechanics

The operational mechanics of Emscripten are worth a closer look. It begins its process by employing Clang, a widely-used open-source compiler, to convert source code written in languages like C and C++ into LLVM bitcode. You might ask, why not compile directly from C/C++ to WASM? The answer lies in the advantages offered by LLVM's intermediate representation. It facilitates cross-platform compatibility and allows for a variety of optimizations, making the ultimate conversion into WebAssembly bytecode more streamlined, effective, and resource-efficient.

Robust Runtime Environment

Emscripten offers more than mere compilation; it provides a robust runtime environment that emulates a full-fledged operating system. This simulation is crucial for the smooth running of C and C++ applications, which often expect various system-level services like file systems, sockets, and more. Emscripten's runtime environment comes equipped with virtual implementations of these system services, allowing a wide range of applications to run without any alterations. For example, if your C application is writing to a file, Emscripten handles this by redirecting the write operation to a virtual in-memory file system, eliminating the need for code modifications when porting to WebAssembly.

Support for SDL and OpenGL

Emscripten has a standout feature in its ability to emulate widely-used multimedia libraries such as SDL and OpenGL. These libraries are essential for a multitude of applications, particularly in gaming, for tasks related to graphics rendering, audio processing, and input handling. Emscripten cleverly translates these library calls into equivalent web technologies like WebGL for graphical rendering and Web Audio API for sound management. This enables a plethora of multimedia applications and games, traditionally confined to desktop environments, to execute efficiently within web browsers.

Customizable HTML Shell

Finally, deploying applications on the web often necessitates an HTML context within which the application resides. Recognizing this, Emscripten offers pre-designed, customizable HTML templates that act as this shell. These templates serve as a container where the compiled WASM code and the associated JavaScript "glue" code reside, giving developers a fully-integrated, deployment-ready web application. This feature alleviates yet another layer of complexity, simplifying the journey for developers keen on webifying their traditional applications.

Applications and Use Cases

Emscripten's flexibility has seen its adoption across a spectrum of applications:

- Gaming: Given its ability to emulate SDL and OpenGL, many games have been ported to the web using Emscripten. This includes both indie titles and classics.

- Scientific Computing: Many scientific applications, written in C or C++, benefit from the web's ubiquity. Emscripten allows these applications to be run in browsers without users needing to install specialized software.

- Education: Emscripten facilitates online interactive coding platforms and playgrounds, especially for languages traditionally considered unsuitable for the web.

- Multimedia Applications: From image editors to video players, Emscripten aids in moving these resource-intensive applications to the browser.

- Legacy Software: Older software, which may no longer run on modern platforms, can find a new lease on life by being ported to the web through Emscripten. This ensures preservation and continued access.

Emscripten's transformative impact is palpable in how we perceive web applications today. It challenges the boundaries of what's achievable in a browser, blurring the lines between native and web applications.

Setting up Emscripten

Emscripten is a powerful tool that revolutionizes how developers perceive and utilize the web. To harness its potential, the first step is a proper installation and configuration in your development environment. This detailed walkthrough will take you through the process, ensuring you're well-equipped to begin your WebAssembly journey.

Before diving in, ensure your system meets the following criteria:

- Emscripten is compatible with macOS, Linux, and Windows.

- Emscripten requires Python. Versions 3.6 to 3.9 are recommended.

- These build tools are necessary for compiling certain components.

- Node.js required for running the test suite and some of the tools Emscripten provides.

Fetching Emscripten SDK

The Emscripten SDK (emsdk) is the gateway to all functionalities Emscripten offers. Fetch it using git:

```
git clone https://github.com/emscripten-core/emsdk.git

cd emsdk
```

This clones the emsdk repository to your local machine, positioning you within the emsdk directory.

Installing SDK Tools

Emscripten is actively developed, and new versions frequently emerge. It's wise to get the latest SDK tools:

```
./emsdk install latest
```

This fetches the latest Emscripten tools, ensuring you're equipped with the most up-to-date capabilities.

Activating SDK Version

After installation, the next step is activating the version:

```
./emsdk activate latest
```

Activation makes this version the default when you invoke Emscripten tools in the terminal. It's pivotal to ensure consistency across projects.

Setting up Environment Variables

Emscripten needs certain environment variables set to function optimally. While the previous command activates the latest version, environment variables aren't automatically set. For this, run:

```
source ./emsdk_env.sh
```

For Windows, use:

```
emsdk_env.bat
```

By executing these, essential paths are appended to your environment variables, granting terminal sessions access to Emscripten commands like emcc.

Testing Installation

A wise developer always verifies their setup. Create a simple C program, hello.c:

```
#include <stdio.h>
```

```c
int main() {
    printf("Hello, Emscripten!\n");
    return 0;
}
```

Compile this with Emscripten:

```
emcc hello.c -o hello.html
```

Emscripten will process hello.c, producing three files:

- hello.html: A shell that loads and runs your application.
- hello.js: The generated JavaScript "glue" code.
- hello.wasm: The compiled WebAssembly module.

Open hello.html in a web browser. You should see the message "Hello, Emscripten!" displayed. If you do, congratulations! Emscripten is functioning correctly.

Configuration File

Emscripten uses a configuration file named .emscripten. Post-installation, this file resides in the user's home directory (or the directory from which Emscripten was run). It contains paths and settings Emscripten requires.

While default settings work for most, advanced users might want to tweak configurations. For instance, altering the LLVM optimizer's aggressiveness or specifying custom system paths. If diving into this, ensure thorough documentation consultation, as misconfigurations can result in compilation failures.

Updating Emscripten

WebAssembly is an evolving ecosystem, and Emscripten keeps pace. Regularly update your Emscripten installation:

```
cd path_to_emsdk/
./emsdk update
./emsdk install latest
```

```
./emsdk activate latest
```

This ensures you leverage the most recent improvements and bug fixes.

Emscripten Ports

Emscripten ports are essential libraries pre-compiled for usage with Emscripten. Examples include zlib, libpng, and SDL2. These are a boon, especially when porting existing applications that rely on such libraries.

To use a port, include it during compilation. For instance:

```
emcc myfile.c -o myfile.html -s USE_SDL=2
```

This instructs Emscripten to link against SDL2 during compilation.

Setting up Emscripten might initially seem daunting, but its rewards are manifold. This toolchain paves the way to transform traditional applications into web-compatible versions, expanding reach and accessibility.

Sample Program: Compiling C++ to WASM

We shall dive into a practical illustration of compiling a C++ program to WebAssembly using Emscripten. This will provide a hands-on grasp of the concepts learned previously.

Demo C++ Program

For this illustration, we shall use a simple C++ program that calculates the factorial of a given number:

```
// factorial.cpp
#include <iostream>

int factorial(int n) {
    if (n <= 1) {
        return 1;
    }
    return n * factorial(n - 1);
}
```

```
int main() {
    int num;
    std::cout << "Enter a number: ";
    std::cin >> num;
    std::cout << "Factorial of " << num << " is " << factorial(num) << std::endl;
    return 0;
}
```

Compilation using Emscripten

Assuming Emscripten is already set up and configured, use the emcc command to compile the C++ file to WebAssembly:

```
emcc factorial.cpp -o factorial.html
```

This command will generate the following files:

- factorial.html: An HTML shell that will be used to run the program in a web browser.
- factorial.js: The JavaScript "glue" code that acts as a bridge between the HTML and the WebAssembly module.
- factorial.wasm: The compiled WebAssembly module.

Run the Program

Simply open the generated factorial.html file in a WebAssembly-compatible web browser. This will display a basic interface where you can enter a number and see the factorial result. Since WebAssembly modules run within a sandboxed environment in the browser, the standard input/output functionalities (like std::cin and std::cout in our example) are handled in a different manner. The default Emscripten HTML shell provides basic I/O functionalities, which is why you'll see an interactive prompt when opening factorial.html. However, in real-world applications, you might want to set up more sophisticated interactions between the browser's DOM and your WebAssembly module. This can be achieved through Emscripten's API, which offers functions to bind C++ classes and methods to JavaScript, enabling richer interactions.

Additional Compilation Flags

Emscripten provides a multitude of flags to control the compilation process.

For example:

- -s WASM=1: Ensures the output is WebAssembly.
- -O3: Applies high-level optimizations to the output.
- --bind: Used when you have C++ bindings you want to expose to JavaScript.

For our simple illustration, the default compilation flags suffice. However, when working on more complex projects, you'll often need to tweak these settings to achieve desired behaviors or optimizations.

Overall, the process of compiling C++ to WebAssembly using Emscripten is straightforward. By writing your program, employing the emcc command for compilation, and then running the resulting HTML file, you can quickly and easily see your C++ code in action within a browser.

Sample Program: Integrating JavaScript

Certainly, integrating JavaScript projects with WebAssembly can unlock powerful computation capabilities. WebAssembly (often abbreviated as wasm) is designed to be a complement to JavaScript, allowing developers to run code written in other languages at near-native speed in the browser. We shall break down how you can seamlessly integrate your JavaScript projects with WebAssembly.

Write a Simple WebAssembly Function

The need to integrate WebAssembly with JavaScript arises from the fact that WebAssembly does not have direct access to the Web APIs provided by browsers. Therefore, any interaction with the DOM or other browser-specific operations must be done through JavaScript.

For our example, we shall compile a simple C function that multiplies two numbers.

```
// multiply.c
int multiply(int a, int b) {
  return a * b;
}
```

Using Emscripten, compile this C code to WebAssembly:

```
emcc multiply.c -o multiply.js -s EXPORTED_FUNCTIONS="['_multiply']"
```

Integrate with JavaScript

After compilation, Emscripten would have produced a multiply.js and a multiply.wasm file. The multiply.js file acts as the glue code, and within it, the WebAssembly module is loaded and initialized.

In your main JavaScript file, you can now integrate this:

```
// main.js
const Module = require('./multiply.js');  // Adjust path accordingly if needed


Module.onRuntimeInitialized = () => {
   const result = Module._multiply(5, 7);  // Use the exported function
   console.log(`The result is: ${result}`); // Outputs: "The result is: 35"
};
```

Notice the onRuntimeInitialized callback. This ensures that the WebAssembly module has been fully loaded and initialized before we try to call any functions from it.

DOM Interactions

WebAssembly, by itself, doesn't have direct access to the DOM. However, with JavaScript as an intermediary, we can achieve this.

For instance, consider an HTML button:

```
<button onclick="multiplyAndDisplay()">Multiply</button>
<div id="output"></div>
You can modify the main.js to include:
function multiplyAndDisplay() {
   const result = Module._multiply(5, 7);
   document.getElementById("output").innerHTML = `The result is: ${result}`;
}
```

Pass Strings and Complex Data

Passing integers or floats between JavaScript and WebAssembly is straightforward. But for strings or more complex data structures, it requires some additional steps:

- Strings: When you need to pass a string from JavaScript to WebAssembly, you need to convert it to a pointer in the WebAssembly module's linear memory.

```
const text = "Hello WebAssembly";
const length = Module.lengthBytesUTF8(text) + 1;
const ptr = Module._malloc(length);
Module.stringToUTF8(text, ptr, length);
```

- Arrays: Similar to strings, arrays need to be copied into WebAssembly memory before they can be used. For instance, if you have an array of integers:

```
const arr = [1, 2, 3, 4, 5];
const data = new Uint8Array(Module.HEAPU8.buffer, Module._malloc(arr.length *
arr.BYTES_PER_ELEMENT), arr.length);
data.set(new Uint8Array(arr.buffer));
```

Free-up Memory

It's vital to free up memory after you're done, especially when manually allocating memory as shown above:

```
Module._free(ptr);
```

Interact with JavaScript Functions

WebAssembly can also call JavaScript functions using Emscripten's EM_JS macro. This is useful when certain functionalities are better handled or can only be handled by JavaScript, like DOM manipulations.

```
#include <emscripten.h>

EM_JS(void, show_alert, (const char* str), {
  alert(UTF8ToString(str));
```

```
});

void myFunction() {
  show_alert("Called from WebAssembly");
}
```

In essence, the marriage of WebAssembly and JavaScript is one of complementary strengths. While WebAssembly brings the power and performance of compiled languages, JavaScript offers ease of use, flexibility, and access to web-specific functionalities. The combined might of both allows developers to craft high-performance web applications that were previously unthinkable in the web domain.

Python and WebAssembly

The synergy of Python—a high-level, dynamic, and versatile language—with WebAssembly, which offers near-native execution speed in browsers, leads us to some intriguing possibilities. WebAssembly was primarily designed for languages with a lower level of abstraction, like C/C++ and Rust. However, with evolving tools and technologies, Python developers are also looking at opportunities to harness the power of WebAssembly. Python, being an interpreted language, can sometimes face challenges in terms of runtime performance, especially in browser environments where JavaScript is the dominant player. WebAssembly offers a chance to bring Python code to the web platform with enhanced performance, especially for compute-intensive tasks.

Python Runtime using Pyodide

One of the most notable projects aiming to bring Python to the WebAssembly landscape is Pyodide. Essentially, Pyodide compiles the Python interpreter to WebAssembly, allowing Python to run in the browser. While not strictly about "compiling" individual Python scripts to wasm, it opens the avenue to run Python in places it couldn't before.

To use Pyodide, you'd typically include it in your web project:

```
<script src="https://pyodide.org/path/to/pyodide.js"></script>
```

Once the Pyodide runtime is loaded, Python code can be executed:

```
// Initialize Pyodide
await loadPyodide({ indexURL : 'https://some-url/' });
```

```
// Execute Python code
let result = pyodide.runPython(`
  import math
  math.sin(math.pi / 2)
`);
console.log(result); // Outputs: 1.0
```

The Pyodide runtime, including the Python standard library and essential packages, can be sizable. This might not be optimal for lightweight web applications.

Transcrypt for JavaScript Transpiler

Another approach to bring Python capabilities to the web is Transcrypt, which transpiles Python code into JavaScript, rather than wasm. By doing so, it allows developers to write Pythonic code for web applications, but it doesn't truly harness the power of WebAssembly.

Transcrypt is used as a command-line tool to convert Python scripts to JavaScript.

```
transcrypt -b -m -n my_python_script.py
```

The result is a JavaScript file that can be included in a web project.

WebAssembly Micro Runtime for Python

For those wanting to truly compile Python to wasm, the WebAssembly Micro Runtime (WAMR) might be of interest. It provides a lightweight standalone wasm runtime with a mini Python interpreter, iwapy, allowing Python bytecode to be executed. It is done easily by simply converting Python code to bytecode, package it with iwapy, then execute it with WAMR. This way, you get a standalone wasm binary running Python code.

Practical Considerations

- Interactivity: When compiling or transpiling Python for the web, consider how the Python code will interact with the web page. Both Pyodide and Transcrypt offer ways for Python to interact with the DOM, but they have their quirks and learning curves.

- Packages: Not all Python packages are available or compatible with these tools. Pyodide, for instance, offers a selection of commonly used packages like NumPy and pandas, but it's not exhaustive. When porting projects, package compatibility needs to be verified.

- Performance Trade-offs: While WebAssembly might boost the performance of certain tasks, it's essential to benchmark and profile the Python code to ensure the conversion process brings tangible benefits.

We may soon see more direct methods of compiling Python to wasm, or even novel approaches to combine Python's expressiveness with WebAssembly's performance. Whether it's running Python directly in the browser with Pyodide, transpiling it to JavaScript with Transcrypt, or harnessing the power of tools like WAMR, Python's presence in the web landscape is set to expand.

WABi Toolkit

Amidst the rapidly evolving landscape of WebAssembly, a number of tools and platforms have been emerging, catering to developers' needs. One of the notable toolkits in this panorama is the WABi Toolkit. The WABi Toolkit (WebAssembly Binary Toolkit) is a comprehensive suite of tools tailored to facilitate the development and integration of WebAssembly applications. It's designed not just for WebAssembly on the web but extends its prowess to server-side and standalone applications, thereby making it a versatile toolkit for a variety of WebAssembly applications.

Key Components of WABi

- WABi Compiler: This component aids in the transformation of high-level programming languages into WebAssembly binaries. While tools like Emscripten focus primarily on C/C++, the WABi Compiler is known for its wider language support.

- WABi Debugger: An instrumental component for developers, this debugger allows for the inspection and debugging of WebAssembly modules, making it easier to identify and resolve issues that may arise during the development phase.

- WABi Runtime: This serves as an execution environment for WebAssembly binaries, supporting a variety of host platforms, which is especially beneficial for applications that aim to run outside the web browser.

Setting up WABi Toolkit

Getting started with WABi is a streamlined process. Following is a stepwise walkthrough to set up the toolkit in your development environment:

- Ensure your system meets the requirements. Typically, the WABi Toolkit supports a variety of operating systems, including Windows, Linux, and macOS. Also, ensure you have a compatible version of Python, as some WABi tools may rely on it.

- Navigate to the official WABi Toolkit website or its GitHub repository. From there, download the latest stable version of the toolkit. While there might be beta or developmental versions available, for production or learning purposes, it's always advisable to go with the stable releases.

- Once downloaded, extract the contents of the toolkit. Depending on your platform, there may be an installer script available. For instance, on Linux, you might find a install.sh script. Execute the following script to install the toolkit:

```
$ ./install.sh
```

For platforms without an installer script, you might need to manually place the toolkit's binaries in a directory included in your system's PATH.

- Some components of the toolkit might require specific environment variables to be set. This is usually documented in the toolkit's setup guide. Ensure you configure these variables as per the documentation to avoid potential issues.

- Once installed, open a terminal or command prompt and test the toolkit by invoking one of its tools. For instance:

```
$ wabi --version
```

- If the command returns the version of the WABi Toolkit, you've successfully set it up.

Remember when we learned using Emscripten for compiling C++ to WebAssembly and subsequently integrating Python with WebAssembly using tools like Pyodide? The WABi Toolkit complements these learnings. While Emscripten and Pyodide have their strengths, WABi brings its own unique capabilities to the table, especially in terms of broader language support and server-side applications. The WABi Toolkit presents a holistic environment for WebAssembly development, from writing code to debugging and deployment.

Compiling Java Apps to WebAssembly

Java, being one of the most popular and versatile programming languages, has fostered a vast ecosystem of applications. As WebAssembly widens its horizon, there's an increasing interest in exploring how existing Java applications can be ported to WebAssembly. While Java bytecode and WebAssembly are distinct, tools have been developed to bridge this gap.

Java applications run on the Java Virtual Machine (JVM), executing bytecode compiled from Java source files. WebAssembly, on the other hand, has its own virtual machine in supported browsers or environments. To run Java in a WebAssembly context, we essentially need a way to convert or interpret Java bytecode within a WebAssembly VM.

TeaVM

TeaVM is one of the foremost tools that allow Java bytecode to be converted into WebAssembly. It's not a JVM; rather, it takes Java bytecode and translates it to JavaScript or WebAssembly, making it runnable in a browser without a traditional Java plugin. Ensure you have Java Development Kit (JDK) installed on your system, as TeaVM requires it. If you're using Maven for your Java project, integrate TeaVM by adding its dependency to your pom.xml:

```
<dependency>
  <groupId>org.teavm</groupId>
  <artifactId>teavm-platform</artifactId>
  <version>0.6.0</version>
</dependency>
```

Once integrated, you can use Maven commands to build and run your project with TeaVM, generating WebAssembly output.

Porting Strategy

When porting a Java application to WebAssembly, consider the following:

- Identify the core computational logic you want to run in WebAssembly. Not all parts of your Java application might be suitable or necessary for WebAssembly.

- Ensure all libraries your Java code depends on are compatible with TeaVM. Some Java libraries may not be supported or may require alternatives.

- WebAssembly modules often need to interact with JavaScript for DOM manipulations or to use browser APIs. TeaVM provides annotations and methods to facilitate this. For example, the @JSExport annotation in TeaVM allows Java methods to be callable from JavaScript.

Sample Program: Java-to-WebAssembly with TeaVM

Consider a simple Java function that computes the factorial of a number:

```
public class Factorial {
   public static long compute(int n) {
      if (n <= 1) return 1;
      return n * compute(n - 1);
   }
}
```

To compile this to WebAssembly, setup a Maven project and integrate TeaVM as mentioned above and annotate the compute method with @JSExport to make it accessible from JavaScript:

```
@JSExport
public static long compute(int n) {...}
```

Then, build the project using Maven. TeaVM will generate the WebAssembly and accompanying JavaScript files. Include the generated files in your HTML and call the factorial function from JavaScript:

```
var result = Factorial_compute(5);
console.log(result); // Outputs 120
```

While TeaVM is powerful, there are some limitations:

- The performance of Java code compiled to WebAssembly might not always match native WebAssembly written in languages like C or Rust. However, for many applications, the performance is more than adequate.

- Java relies on garbage collection for memory management. When running in WebAssembly, TeaVM provides its own simplified garbage collector. This may have implications for applications with high memory churn.

- Not all Java features and libraries are supported. For instance, Java's reflection capabilities are limited in TeaVM.

While our focus has been on running Java in the browser via WebAssembly, there's potential beyond this realm. With the advent of WebAssembly runtimes like WASI (WebAssembly System Interface), it's possible to run WebAssembly modules, including those compiled from Java, outside the browser in server-side environments or even IoT devices.

Connecting with our prior learnings, especially around WABi Toolkit and Emscripten, it's evident that the landscape of tools bridging high-level languages with WebAssembly is diverse. TeaVM stands out in the domain of Java, offering a way to leverage the vast Java ecosystem in the realm of WebAssembly. In essence, as WebAssembly continues its upward trajectory in the world of web and beyond, tools like TeaVM open doors for leveraging existing Java assets.

WebAssembly Bindings

One of the compelling features of WebAssembly is its ability to run in tandem with JavaScript, leveraging web APIs and accessing DOM. However, this interaction between WebAssembly and JavaScript isn't direct. This is where WebAssembly bindings come into play. Bindings serve as the connectors that enable smooth interaction between WebAssembly modules and the surrounding JavaScript or web environment. WebAssembly bindings refer to libraries or tool-generated code that allows WebAssembly modules to interact seamlessly with the host environment, primarily the JavaScript runtime in browsers.

These bindings facilitate:

- Calling WebAssembly functions from JavaScript and vice versa.

- Passing complex data types between JavaScript and WebAssembly.

- Handling JavaScript objects or web APIs within WebAssembly code.

Tools for Creating Bindings

There are several tools that aid in generating bindings, and some of them include:

- Emscripten: A toolchain we previously touched upon, Emscripten not only compiles C/C++ to WebAssembly but also generates the necessary bindings for the resultant WASM to interact with JavaScript.

- wasm-bindgen: Specifically designed for Rust, wasm-bindgen facilitates high-level interactions between Rust-generated WebAssembly and JavaScript.

Sample Program: Using Bindings

To understand bindings in depth, we shall consider a scenario involving the calculation of factorials. While we previously computed factorials using Java and C++, we shall explore this with Rust, showcasing how wasm-bindgen aids in the interaction between WebAssembly and JavaScript.

Create a factorial calculator in Rust, compile it to WebAssembly, and then use it in a JavaScript environment with the help of bindings.

Rust Code for Factorial Calculation

```
use wasm_bindgen::prelude::*;

#[wasm_bindgen]
pub fn factorial(n: i32) -> i32 {
  if n <= 1 { return 1; }
  n * factorial(n - 1)
}
```

Note the use of the #[wasm_bindgen] attribute. This indicates that the factorial function should be accessible from JavaScript once compiled to WebAssembly.

Compiling Rust to WebAssembly with Bindings

Using the Rust toolchain, and particularly wasm-pack, you can compile the Rust code into WebAssembly and generate the necessary bindings:

```
$ wasm-pack build
```

This command generates a pkg directory containing the WebAssembly binary and the corresponding JavaScript binding.

Integrating with JavaScript

Once the bindings and WebAssembly module are generated, you can integrate them into your JavaScript application:

```
import { factorial } from "./pkg/factorial_module";

const result = factorial(5);
console.log(result); // Outputs: 120
```

Advantages of WebAssembly Bindings

- One of the most striking advantages of using WebAssembly bindings is the unparalleled flexibility it offers developers. These bindings act as a bridge, allowing you to merge the raw speed and performance of WebAssembly code with the unparalleled versatility and ease of use of JavaScript. This means you're not constrained to choose between the two; instead, you can leverage the best aspects of both.

- Another considerable advantage is the ability for code reusability. With the right bindings in place, pre-existing WebAssembly modules can be easily integrated into a multitude of JavaScript applications without much hassle. This saves time and effort as you don't have to re-invent the wheel, leading to quicker deployment and less redundant code.

- Perhaps the most technically intriguing advantage is interoperability. WebAssembly bindings allow for the exchange of complex data types, intricate structures, and even intricate functions between JavaScript and WebAssembly environments. This makes it possible to perform more advanced operations and build more complex applications than would be possible with either technology in isolation.

Challenges and Points of Caution

- Although WebAssembly bindings offer seamless interaction between JavaScript and WebAssembly, there can be performance costs. Specifically, a certain degree of performance overhead might be incurred when there is frequent switching between the two contexts. This overhead may be negligible for some applications but could become a bottleneck in performance-critical scenarios.

- Memory Management: Especially for those using languages like C and C++, which require manual memory management, care must be taken. When WebAssembly and JavaScript are both accessing the same resources, the correct allocation and deallocation of these shared resources become crucial to avoid memory leaks or crashes. Understanding and managing the lifecycle of objects and memory in both contexts is essential.

- When applications demand parallel processing or concurrent operations, synchronized access to shared resources becomes exceedingly important. Failure to ensure this synchronization between JavaScript and WebAssembly contexts can lead to unexpected behavior, data races, or even application crashes. Therefore, you'll need to carefully implement locks or other synchronization primitives to coordinate access to shared resources.

Recalling our earlier learnings on event-driven microservices in WebAssembly and handling errors, imagine if you wished to expose a WebAssembly function that processes events and logs errors. With the appropriate bindings, you can call this function from JavaScript, pass it an event object, and let it return a result or error message. The binding ensures that the event object from JavaScript is correctly interpreted in WebAssembly and vice versa.

WebAssembly Error Handling and Solutions

While diving into WebAssembly, its bindings, compilation with Emscripten, and integration into diverse languages, there are several pitfalls a developer might encounter. We shall learn some common issues, their potential causes, and practical solutions.

Module Failed to Instantiate

This error occurs when trying to instantiate a WebAssembly module using the WebAssembly JavaScript API.

Cause

The WebAssembly binary might be corrupted, or there could be a missing import during instantiation.

Solution

Ensure your WebAssembly binary is correctly generated. If using Emscripten, ensure all necessary flags and options are correctly set. If the error persists, check the imports you're providing during instantiation. For example:

```
WebAssembly.instantiate(wasmModule, {
  env: {
    // Ensure all necessary functions are provided here
  }
});
```

Memory Out-of-Bounds

This error pops up when trying to access memory locations that are not within the allocated WebAssembly memory.

Cause

Trying to read/write outside the defined linear memory.

Solution

Ensure all memory accesses are within the defined range. Check your source code for array overflows or underflows. For C/C++, it could look like:

```
int arr[5];
arr[6] = 10; // Out-of-bounds access
```

Function Signature Mismatch

This indicates a discrepancy between the expected function signature in WebAssembly and what's provided in JavaScript.

Cause

Mismatch in function parameters or return type.

Solution

Ensure the function signatures match. For example, if WebAssembly expects a function add(int, int) -> int, the JavaScript function should look like:

```
function add(x, y) {
  return x + y;
}
```

Type Mismatch when using Bindings

While using tools like wasm-bindgen, you might find errors regarding type mismatches.

Cause

Passing incompatible data types between JavaScript and WebAssembly.

Solution

Ensure data types match. For Rust and JavaScript:

```
#[wasm_bindgen]
pub fn greet(name: String) {
    // ...
}

// JavaScript
import { greet } from "./wasm_module";
greet("Alice");
```

Compilation Failures with Emscripten

Sometimes, while compiling code to WebAssembly using Emscripten, you might face compilation errors.

Cause

Syntax errors, missing libraries, or wrong compiler flags.

Solution

Ensure your source code is error-free. When using Emscripten, check for any missing libraries and ensure the right flags are set. For instance:

```
emcc source.c -s WASM=1 -o output.html
```

WebAssembly Module Size too Large

When working with extensive projects, you might end up with a considerably large WebAssembly binary.

Cause

Inclusion of unnecessary libraries, not optimizing the compilation.

Solution

Use Emscripten's optimization flags and exclude any unused libraries. For example:

```
emcc source.c -s WASM=1 -O3 -o output.html
```

Python/Java to WebAssembly Conversion Issues

While porting Python or Java applications to WebAssembly, there can be issues like missing functionalities or performance discrepancies.

Cause

These can be due to the inherent differences in the runtime environments of these languages compared to WebAssembly.

Solution

Ensure that you're using tools specifically designed for these languages, like Pyodide for Python. Limit the use of native libraries or functionalities that might not have a direct counterpart in WebAssembly.

Bindings Not Working as Expected

Even after generating bindings using tools like wasm-bindgen, you might find that the integration isn't smooth.

Cause

Inaccuracies in binding definitions or in the way they're being used.

Solution

Thoroughly check the generated binding code. Ensure that you're using the latest versions of the tools. Also, remember to regenerate bindings whenever there's a change in the source code.

WebAssembly Thread Synchronization Issues

When working with WebAssembly threads, you might face issues related to concurrent data access or unexpected behaviors.

Cause

Inaccurate use of synchronization primitives or misunderstanding of the concurrency model.

Solution

Ensure you're using atomic operations, mutexes, or other synchronization primitives accurately. Ensure shared memory regions are appropriately protected from concurrent modifications.

Summary

In this chapter, we dove headfirst into the vast world of WebAssembly tools and interoperability to get a better understanding of both topics. To begin, we began by deciphering the core of Emscripten, which is a leading toolchain for compiling codebases written in C and C++, amongst other languages, into WebAssembly. Emscripten provides a comprehensive environment that encapsulates the complexities of WebAssembly. As a result, it is much simpler for developers to take advantage of the performance benefits offered by this bytecode. We discovered the steps necessary to install Emscripten, configure it, and integrate it seamlessly into an existing development environment by using practical walkthroughs to uncover these steps.

The demonstration of compiling a C++ programme to WebAssembly, which showed off the ease of use and effectiveness brought about by Emscripten, was a major high point of the event. After that, we moved on to integrating JavaScript and WebAssembly into the system. Given the widespread adoption of JavaScript across the modern web ecosystem, having a solid grasp of this integration is of the utmost importance. Developers have the ability to combine the flexibility of JavaScript with the speed of WebAssembly if there is smooth interoperability between the two. In addition, the chapter expanded its learning of interoperability to include Python, which is a widely used programming language that is well-known for being easy to learn and having an extensive library ecosystem. We navigated the complexities and nuances of porting Python projects to WebAssembly, elaborating on the strategic importance of tools such as Pyodide in bridging the gap between the two very different environments.

After that, we turned our attention to the WABi toolkit, illuminating its capabilities and providing specifics regarding its configuration. The development of this toolkit, which is capable of converting Java bytecode into WebAssembly, is illustrative of the broadening scope of applications for WebAssembly. After that, the chapter moved on to learn WebAssembly bindings, which are an important component of the process of integrating WebAssembly modules into their respective host environments, such as web browsers or server-side applications. We gained an understanding of the binding scenarios and their respective implementations through the use of practical examples. To sum up, our trip was not devoid of any difficulties along the way. We dissected the potential blunders and problems that could arise within this enormous ecosystem, and as a result, we are now armed with the knowledge and solutions necessary to prevent these problems from occurring or to quickly resolve them.

By the time we reach the end of this chapter, we will have acquired a comprehensive understanding of the multifaceted WebAssembly ecosystem, including its toolchains as well as its capabilities for seamless integration across a variety of programming languages. In combination with strategic insights, the hands-on approaches provide software developers with the expertise necessary to exploit the full potential of WebAssembly in a wide variety of applications.

Chapter 5: Advanced WebAssembly Tools and Techniques

Introduction to Binaryen

In the vast landscape of WebAssembly (Wasm), certain tools and compilers stand out, and Binaryen is one of them. As we venture into the intricacies of WebAssembly's world, understanding the tools that power this ecosystem is of paramount importance. Binaryen is a compiler and toolchain infrastructure library specifically designed for WebAssembly, offering various functionalities that range from optimizing Wasm binaries to providing compiler middle-end functionalities. We shall delve deeper to unveil the capabilities and utilities of Binaryen and how it complements and enriches the WebAssembly domain.

Binaryen, at its core, is an optimizer for WebAssembly. Its name, derived from "binary" and the suffix "-en", gives a hint at its primary function. It works on the WebAssembly binaries, optimizing and transforming them to be smaller and more efficient. This not only aids in faster downloads of Wasm modules but also ensures that they execute more rapidly on the client side. However, Binaryen is not just limited to optimization. Its versatile nature makes it a favorite amongst developers. It offers a C API, which allows for integration with other projects. The C API also acts as a bridge, enabling manipulations and transformations of Wasm modules in other languages, facilitating a broader reach and interoperability.

Components of Binaryen

Binaryen comes bundled with a variety of tools, each tailored for specific tasks:

wasm-opt

This tool stands out as perhaps the most renowned utility within the entire Binaryen toolkit. Its primary focus is on the optimization of WebAssembly binaries. It meticulously trims down unnecessary code and streamlines the binaries, making them not just smaller in size but also significantly more efficient in terms of execution speed.

wasm-as and wasm-dis

These twin tools serve as the backbone for format conversion operations involving WebAssembly code. The wasm-as tool takes text-format WebAssembly code and converts it into its binary counterpart, enabling easier distribution and faster loading times. On the other hand, wasm-dis performs the reverse operation; it takes binary-format WebAssembly code and converts it into its text-based representation. This text-based format is easier to read and proves to be invaluable during debugging sessions or when one needs to perform code analysis.

wasm-shell

Specifically designed with testing scenarios in mind, wasm-shell facilitates the execution of WebAssembly code within a shell-like environment. This sandboxed area allows developers to run their WebAssembly code snippets and inspect their behavior in isolation, aiding immensely in the debugging and validation phases of the development cycle.

wasm2js

Serving a unique but crucial role, the wasm2js tool can translate WebAssembly code into JavaScript code. Although doing so inevitably results in some level of performance degradation due to the translation overhead, the tool proves indispensable when you need backward compatibility for platforms or browsers that do not natively support WebAssembly.

Each of these tools, with their specialized functionalities, combine to form a comprehensive toolkit in Binaryen that empowers developers to more efficiently write, debug, optimize, and understand WebAssembly code.

Role of Binaryen in WebAssembly

WebAssembly aims to execute at near-native speed, and Binaryen assists in achieving this objective by carrying out following functions:

- Optimization Techniques: Binaryen employs various sophisticated optimization techniques, some shared with traditional compilers, and some unique to WebAssembly's characteristics. These techniques, such as dead code elimination, local simplifications, and redundant code removal, ensure that the final Wasm binary is devoid of unnecessary bulk.

- Facilitating Debugging: The ability to disassemble WebAssembly binaries into a human-readable text format is crucial during the development phase. Binaryen's tools like wasm-dis allow developers to inspect and debug the code, ensuring that the deployed Wasm modules are error-free.

- Interoperability and Compatibility: In situations where platforms might not support WebAssembly, tools like wasm2js ensure that Wasm code can still run by converting it to JavaScript. This ensures a broader reach and guarantees that applications remain functional across diverse platforms.

- Compiler Middle-end Functionalities: Apart from just acting as an optimizer, Binaryen also provides compiler middle-end functionalities. This means it can take in a high-level representation of code, optimize it, and produce a low-level representation, ready to be converted to machine code. This has proven particularly beneficial in projects where Binaryen has been used as a target for compiler backends.

- Binaryen and Emscripten: While Binaryen is powerful in its own right, its collaboration with Emscripten, amplifies its capabilities. Emscripten, known for converting C/C++

codebases into WebAssembly, employs Binaryen for the optimization of the final Wasm output. This collaboration ensures that the Wasm modules generated are not just functionally accurate but are also optimized for performance.

Setting up Binaryen and Emscripten Integration

Binaryen, as we learned, is a pivotal instrument in the WebAssembly orchestra, enabling optimization, analysis, and multiple manipulations of WebAssembly code. This extensive detailed walkthrough will walk you through the process of integrating Binaryen with your current environment and ensuring it cooperates seamlessly with Emscripten.

Installing Binaryen

From Source

To fetch the latest Binaryen code, you'll need Git. Clone the Binaryen repository:

```
git clone https://github.com/WebAssembly/binaryen.git
```

Now, navigate to the cloned directory:

```
cd binaryen
```

To build Binaryen, utilize CMake:

```
cmake . && make
```

This will build the Binaryen tools and libraries. If the process completes without issues, you'll have Binaryen binaries in the bin/ directory of the cloned repository.

Using Package Managers

Depending on your operating system, there are simpler routes to installing Binaryen:

For macOS users with Homebrew:

```
brew install binaryen
```

For Ubuntu users (or similar Linux distributions):

```
sudo apt-get install binaryen
```

Integrating Binaryen with Emscripten

Emscripten often bundles a version of Binaryen. However, if you need the latest features of Binaryen or want to ensure both tools are perfectly in sync, ensure that both Emscripten and Binaryen are installed and functional. Then, modify the .emscripten configuration file. This file is usually located in your home directory. Within this file, locate the BINARYEN_ROOT variable and point it to the directory where you've installed or built Binaryen. For instance:

```
BINARYEN_ROOT = '/path/to/binaryen'
```

To ensure the integration has been successful, you can run the Emscripten compiler (emcc) with the --show-commands option. This should display commands involving Binaryen tools like wasm-opt.

Using Binaryen to Port Python Programs

The process of using Binaryen to directly compile Python code to WebAssembly isn't straightforward since Binaryen doesn't natively support Python to WASM conversion. It works with intermediary representations, like asm.js, to transform them into WebAssembly. In our previous sections, we had mentioned tools like Pyodide, which use Emscripten under the hood. Emscripten itself utilizes Binaryen for some optimization steps.

However, for our learning purposes, we can demonstrate a roundabout way using C or C++ as an intermediary:

Convert Python to C++

First, we need to represent our Python code in C or C++. For instance, our hypothetical Python code:

```
def greet(name):
    return "Hello, " + name + "!"
```

Can be translated to C++ as:

```
#include <iostream>
#include <string>

std::string greet(std::string name) {
```

```
    return "Hello, " + name + "!";
}

int main() {
    std::string name = "World";
    std::cout << greet(name) << std::endl;
    return 0;
}
```

Compile C++ to WebAssembly

Binaryen includes a tool called wasm-c-api which is a C API for the WebAssembly binary format and execution. But direct C++ to WASM compilation using Binaryen isn't its primary use case. Instead, we'd use Emscripten to compile C++ to WebAssembly and then use Binaryen for optimization.

First, using Emscripten:

```
emcc greet.cpp -o greet.js -s WASM=1
```

This will give us greet.wasm and a greet.js. Now, to optimize the WebAssembly using Binaryen's wasm-opt:

```
wasm-opt greet.wasm -O3 -o greet-optimized.wasm
```

The -O3 flag represents a high level of optimization.

Integration with Web

Now that we have our optimized WASM file, we can integrate it with a web page. The previously generated greet.js will serve as the "glue" code.

```
<!DOCTYPE html>
<html lang="en">
<head>
    <meta charset="UTF-8">
    <meta name="viewport" content="width=device-width, initial-scale=1.0">
    <title>Python to WebAssembly via Binaryen</title>
```

```
</head>
<body>
  <script src="greet.js"></script>
  <script>
    Module.onRuntimeInitialized = function() {
      let greetFunc = Module.cwrap('greet', 'string', ['string']);
      console.log(greetFunc('World'));
    }
  </script>
</body>
</html>
```

Run this in a server environment to avoid cross-origin restrictions that browsers apply when reading local files. It's worth noting that this process is a bit convoluted. Directly compiling Python to WebAssembly through C/C++ involves multiple transformations, each adding its own layer of abstraction. This is not the most efficient way to run Python code in the browser. However, the exercise demonstrates the flexibility of the toolchain available for WebAssembly and how tools like Binaryen fit into this ecosystem. For Python developers, leveraging tools dedicated to bringing Python to the web, like Pyodide, is generally more practical and efficient.

Binaryen for Optimization

Binaryen is primarily an optimizer and intermediary toolset for WebAssembly, providing compilers, optimizers, and related infrastructure. Its role in optimizing WebAssembly code is particularly invaluable, especially for developers aiming to push the performance boundaries of their applications.

For the sake of demonstration, we shall take an intricate program, a C++ code, which we learned when learning about Emscripten. Suppose this code performs matrix multiplication, a compute-intensive task, and we want to ensure the WebAssembly version is as optimized as possible.

Matrix Multiplication

```
#include <iostream>
#include <vector>

using namespace std;
```

```
typedef vector<vector<int>> Matrix;

Matrix multiplyMatrices(const Matrix &a, const Matrix &b) {
    int n = a.size();
    Matrix result(n, vector<int>(n, 0));

    for (int i = 0; i < n; i++) {
        for (int j = 0; j < n; j++) {
            for (int k = 0; k < n; k++) {
                result[i][j] += a[i][k] * b[k][j];
            }
        }
    }
    return result;
}

int main() {
    Matrix a = {{1, 2}, {3, 4}};
    Matrix b = {{2, 0}, {1, 3}};
    Matrix result = multiplyMatrices(a, b);

    for (int i = 0; i < result.size(); i++) {
        for (int j = 0; j < result[i].size(); j++) {
            cout << result[i][j] << " ";
        }
        cout << endl;
    }
    return 0;
}
```

Compiling this code with Emscripten would look something like:

```
emcc matrix_multiplication.cpp -o matrix.html -s WASM=1
```

This would produce matrix.wasm and accompanying JavaScript bindings.

Optimization with Binaryen

Once you have the .wasm file, Binaryen can be used to optimize it further. The wasm-opt tool in the Binaryen suite is specifically designed for this.

```
wasm-opt matrix.wasm -O4 -o matrix_optimized.wasm
```

Here, -O4 is an aggressive optimization level which includes loop unrolling and inlining, suitable for compute-heavy tasks like matrix multiplication.

We shall learn the potential optimizations:

- Inlining: This process replaces function calls with the actual code of the function being called. For smaller functions that are called repeatedly, this can eliminate the overhead of the function call.

- Dead Code Elimination: Removes code that doesn't contribute to the final output. For instance, if there were auxiliary functions or variables we didn't use in the final matrix multiplication version, they'd be pruned.

- Loop Unrolling: It's a technique where the loop's body is duplicated to decrease the overhead of the loop control. Given our triple nested loop for matrix multiplication, this could be especially beneficial.

- Constant Propagation and Folding: If there are constants, the optimizer would evaluate expressions at compile time, reducing work during execution.

- Simplification: Redundant or repeated operations can be identified and simplified.

Web Integration of Optimized WASM

Post optimization, you'll integrate the WebAssembly code similarly. However, the critical difference is you'd use the matrix_optimized.wasm instead of the original matrix.wasm. The generated JS bindings remain the same, ensuring the optimized WASM module interoperates seamlessly with the web application.

Summary

Binaryen emerged as a critical toolset in the WebAssembly ecosystem, serving as an optimizer and intermediary platform for WebAssembly. Its suite of tools, including compilers, optimizers, and related infrastructure utilities, empowers developers to elevate the performance of their WebAssembly applications. By comprehensively understanding Binaryen's capabilities, we unearthed its potential in optimizing WebAssembly code, making it an invaluable asset for developers aiming to refine the efficiency of their applications.

Setting up Binaryen proved to be straightforward. By leveraging specific package managers or compiling from source, developers can quickly integrate Binaryen into their development environment. Notably, its seamless compatibility with Emscripten (a toolchain we learned earlier) became evident. Once integrated with Emscripten, Binaryen augments the process of compiling various programming languages to WebAssembly, streamlining the development pipeline.

Through hands-on exercises, we dived deep into Binaryen's practical applications. Using its tools, especially wasm-opt, we explored how to refine the performance of WebAssembly modules. By applying aggressive optimization levels, we witnessed transformations like inlining, loop unrolling, and dead code elimination in action. These procedures, especially when applied to compute-intensive tasks, can drastically enhance application performance. Nevertheless, while optimization offers numerous benefits, it's essential to approach it judiciously, weighing the trade-offs between runtime efficiency and factors like binary size.

Binaryen's versatility shone as we navigated its interoperability with various languages. For instance, by utilizing Binaryen, we compiled Python programs into WebAssembly and optimized complex C++ programs, highlighting Binaryen's capabilities in diverse scenarios. Moreover, as we explored WebAssembly bindings, the concept of establishing connections between WebAssembly and other languages became clear, accentuating the adaptability and broad applicability of WebAssembly in modern web development.

Chapter 6: Advanced Performance Optimization

Up until this point, we have covered both the fundamentals of WebAssembly as well as a variety of its more complex aspects. After establishing a foundational understanding of it, we proceeded to investigate its benefits, toolkits, and the ways in which it integrates with a variety of programming languages such as C++, Python, and Java. We have mastered concepts such as Emscripten, WABi toolkit, and Binaryen through the use of practical examples. Additionally, we have mastered techniques for memory management and performance optimisation. Each chapter equipped us with the knowledge necessary to compile WebAssembly code, optimise it, and incorporate it into a variety of projects.

As we prepare to move on to Chapter 6, we are getting ready to delve more deeply into specialised areas that can have a significant impact on the performance of WebAssembly applications. This chapter provides a comprehensive look into performance optimisation, covering a wide range of topics including profiling and benchmarking of WebAssembly codes, fine-tuning memory management, and more. In addition to that, we will investigate multi-threading and parallelism, as well as learn how to maximise the performance of networks and browsers. The course will cover a variety of topics, including code splitting, caching strategies, and lazy loading, in addition to demonstrating how to use WebAssembly in conjunction with Web Workers and GPU Acceleration.

WebAssembly Performance Overview

Profiling and Benchmarking WASM

Profiling and benchmarking are foundational in evaluating WebAssembly's performance. By analyzing the runtime behavior of the code, developers identify bottlenecks and areas of improvement. Benchmarking, on the other hand, measures the performance metrics of the WebAssembly modules, allowing comparison against alternative implementations or versions. Both processes serve as a compass, directing developers to optimize their WebAssembly applications methodically.

Fine-tuning Memory Management

Memory management remains a critical facet of WebAssembly. Since WebAssembly operates within a linear memory model, memory allocation, deallocation, and garbage collection become pivotal. Fine-tuning these aspects ensures that applications utilize memory efficiently, thereby preventing leaks and redundant allocations. An efficient memory management approach boosts application speed and reliability.

Leveraging Browser Performance Tools

Modern browsers come packed with a suite of developer tools, and these can be extended to profile, debug, and optimize WebAssembly applications. Using tools like Chrome DevTools or Firefox's Web Developer suite, developers can peek into WebAssembly's performance in a real-world environment, revealing insights that might be elusive in isolated testing environments.

Multi-threading and Parallelism

With the web platform's evolution, utilizing multi-threaded operations and parallel processing has become possible, even within WebAssembly. By exploiting multi-core CPUs and implementing parallel algorithms, WebAssembly applications can process data more swiftly, especially for tasks like image processing, simulations, and data analysis.

Optimizing Network Performance

Given that WebAssembly applications often need to fetch modules over the network, reducing the size of these modules and ensuring efficient transfer mechanisms become essential. Techniques like compression, differential serving, and efficient encoding can drastically reduce load times, offering users a snappier experience.

Lazy Loading and Code Splitting

Instead of loading the entire WebAssembly module at once, developers can leverage lazy loading to fetch only the necessary parts of the application on demand. Paired with code splitting, which breaks the application into smaller chunks, these techniques can enhance the application's perceived and actual load times, improving user experience.

Caching Strategies and WebAssembly

Caching is a time-tested strategy to expedite access to frequently used data. By efficiently caching WebAssembly modules, developers can avoid redundant network requests. This involves using techniques like Service Workers or browser cache to store modules locally, ensuring that repeat visits to a web page are blazing fast.

Web Workers

Web Workers allow scripts to run in the background, separate from the main browser thread. When combined with WebAssembly, this means computationally intensive tasks can be offloaded, preventing the main thread from becoming blocked. This leads to smoother animations and user interactions, even when heavy processing is underway.

GPU Acceleration

The power of the Graphics Processing Unit (GPU) isn't just for graphics. General-purpose GPU (GPGPU) programming allows WebAssembly applications to offload certain tasks to the GPU, harnessing its parallel processing capabilities. For specific types of operations, especially those involving matrices or large data sets, GPU acceleration can provide a substantial performance uplift.

In this chapter, you will delve deep into each of these topics, unraveling the potential of WebAssembly and the strategies to harness its maximum capability. Through a mix of theoretical insights and practical demonstrations, you will explore how to craft WebAssembly applications that are not only performant but also efficient and user-friendly.

Profiling and Benchmarking WebAssembly

When venturing into the realm of WebAssembly, it's vital to appreciate that, like any other software paradigm, WebAssembly isn't immune to performance pitfalls. To ensure that applications maintain a robust performance profile, developers must engage in proactive profiling and benchmarking exercises. While these terms are often used interchangeably in colloquial conversations, they serve distinct purposes in the optimization landscape.

Profiling

Profiling is analogous to a diagnostic tool used by developers to glean insights into the runtime behavior of an application. By using a profiler, developers can see a magnified view of their application's runtime dynamics, revealing how the system resources, especially CPU and memory, interact with the WebAssembly code.

Following are the core aspects of profiling:

- Resource Consumption: At its core, profiling highlights the resource consumption metrics. How much CPU time does a particular function use? How does memory allocation vary across different WebAssembly modules? Answers to these questions can expose inefficiencies.

- Call Stacks: Profilers offer insights into the call stacks, helping developers understand the hierarchy and sequence of function calls. Spotting recursive calls or functions that are invoked more frequently than expected can be instrumental in refining the code.

- Hotspots: These are the segments of the code where the application spends a disproportionate amount of time. Identifying hotspots allows developers to focus their optimization efforts on areas that will yield the most significant performance gains.

Benchmarking

While profiling provides a detailed view of an application's behavior, benchmarking aims to measure its performance under defined conditions. It's about obtaining quantifiable metrics, which can be compared against a standard, previous iterations of the same application, or rival implementations.

Following are the core aspects of benchmarking:

- Standardized Tests: Benchmarking necessitates the use of standardized tests, ensuring consistency. These tests should simulate real-world scenarios, ensuring the derived metrics are relevant and actionable.
- Iterative Process: Benchmarking isn't a one-off task. It's an iterative process where developers continually measure performance, implement optimizations, and then measure again. This cycle helps in tracking improvements or regressions.
- Comparative Analysis: Once benchmarks are run, the data is often compared either against past performance metrics of the same application or against industry standards. This comparison helps in understanding where the application stands in the broader ecosystem.

The Symbiotic Relationship

While both profiling and benchmarking serve unique roles, they're often used in tandem. Profiling identifies areas that need improvement, and benchmarking quantifies this need. Once optimizations are implemented based on profiling insights, benchmarking measures the impact of these changes, creating a feedback loop that's crucial for performance-driven development.

For instance, a developer might notice through profiling that a specific function in a WebAssembly module consumes a significant chunk of CPU time. Post-optimization, benchmarking can then measure if this function's execution time has indeed decreased and by what margin. Given WebAssembly's promise of near-native performance on the web, there's an inherent expectation of efficiency. However, achieving this efficiency isn't serendipitous. It requires rigorous profiling to understand the application's intricacies and robust benchmarking to ensure that the application not only feels fast but is, in measurable terms, truly performant.

Sample Program: Execute Profiling and Benchmark

Profiling and benchmarking your WebAssembly code can provide invaluable insights into your application's performance. We shall walk through a practical approach using one of the previously learned examples, a WebAssembly module compiled from C++ using Emscripten.

Profiling WebAssembly with Chrome DevTools

For this section, we shall take the earlier example of a WebAssembly module that performs mathematical computations.

Setting up Environment

- Ensure you have Chrome installed.
- Run your WebAssembly-enabled web application.

Open Chrome DevTools

- Right-click on your web page and select 'Inspect', or use Ctrl+Shift+I.
- Navigate to the 'Performance' tab.

Record a Profile

- Click the 'Start recording' button (the circle).
- While recording, execute the WebAssembly function in your application, preferably multiple times to capture more data.
- Click 'Stop recording'.

Analyze the Data

- You'll see a timeline of events. Zoom in on areas with high activity.
- Under the 'Main' thread, look for your WebAssembly module. This will provide you with information on how much time is spent executing specific functions within your module.

Benchmarking using JavaScript

- To benchmark, you'll want to measure the execution time of your WebAssembly function(s). You will use the performance.now() function for precise timing in JavaScript.
- Using our mathematical computation example:

// Assuming the WebAssembly module is already instantiated and named 'wasmModule'

```
const startTime = performance.now();

// Call your WebAssembly function multiple times to get an average
for (let i = 0; i < 1000; i++) {
  wasmModule._yourFunctionName(); // Replace with your function's name
}

const endTime = performance.now();

const averageTime = (endTime - startTime) / 1000;

console.log(`Average execution time: ${averageTime} ms`);
```

- This script will execute your WebAssembly function 1000 times and provide you with an average execution time.

Tips for Effective Profiling and Benchmarking

- Ensure that your environment remains consistent between runs. Close other applications and browser tabs, and ensure no background processes are using significant resources.
- Always run your benchmarks multiple times. This helps in averaging out minor variations and provides a more accurate picture.
- If you're particularly interested in a specific function or section of your code, try to isolate it when profiling or benchmarking. This can give you a clearer view of its performance impact.
- After you've made optimizations based on your profiling and benchmarking results, always go back and run the tests again. This iterative approach ensures your changes resulted in the desired performance improvements.

Following these steps and tips, you'll gain a deeper understanding of how your WebAssembly code performs. This knowledge, in turn, can guide your optimization efforts, ensuring your applications run smoothly and efficiently.

Fine-Tune Memory Management

The memory model functions as a continuous block of bytes, similar to how an array operates. This contiguous memory space is accessible not only to the WebAssembly modules but also to the JavaScript runtime environment, thereby providing a common ground for data interaction and manipulation between the two. The underlying principle here is straightforward: unlike traditional systems that manage memory using distinct objects, structures, or linked lists, WebAssembly relies on a singular linear memory space to facilitate both code and data storage.

By default, WebAssembly memory is static, meaning it does not expand or shrink during runtime. Consequently, if a WebAssembly module tries to access or allocate memory beyond the pre-defined limits, it will trigger an error. However, developers have the option to enable dynamic memory growth, which does come with its own set of trade-offs. While enabling memory growth safeguards against running out of memory space, it can lead to issues such as memory fragmentation and other inefficiencies, impacting overall performance.

Memory in WebAssembly can be pre-populated or initialized using what is known as data segments. Data segments are specific portions or chunks of data that are embedded directly into the WebAssembly binary. These segments are then loaded into the allocated memory block when the WebAssembly module is initialized or instantiated. Through careful planning, organization, and optimization of these data segments, developers can effectively manage and even enhance how memory is utilized within the WebAssembly environment.

The way your WebAssembly code interacts with and accesses this linear memory can significantly influence the program's performance. For example, sequential memory access is typically quicker than random memory access. This is primarily because CPUs are designed to cache memory, and sequential access aligns well with this caching mechanism, thereby increasing data retrieval speeds.

One of the unique characteristics of WebAssembly is its absence of a built-in garbage collector. While this omission leads to faster execution times—since there are no interruptions due to garbage collection processes—it also imposes a responsibility on developers for manual memory management. This task entails the explicit allocation and deallocation of memory blocks, usually using tools, libraries, or utilities that are supplied by the programming language from which the WebAssembly code was originally compiled.

Strategies for Efficient Memory Management

- Memory Pooling: Allocating memory in chunks (or pools) can help reduce the overhead and time spent on frequent allocations and deallocations. By reusing these chunks for different data as needed, memory pooling can enhance both speed and memory utilization.

- Minimizing Global Variables: Reducing the usage of global variables can help in conserving memory, especially when these variables remain unused for extended periods.

- Optimize Data Structures: Employing compact data structures, especially in frequently accessed parts of the code, can have a profound impact. For instance, using arrays instead of linked lists in scenarios where random access is frequent can be beneficial.

- Stack and Heap Management: The stack, used for static memory allocation, is managed automatically. In contrast, the heap, used for dynamic memory allocation, requires manual intervention. Balancing and optimizing the use of stack and heap memory can lead to more efficient memory utilization.

- Compressing Data: For applications dealing with significant data (like graphics), compressing data before storing it in memory and decompressing it only when required can help in efficient memory utilization.

- Active Monitoring: Regularly monitoring memory usage during development can catch inefficiencies early. Tools that provide insights into memory allocation, deallocation, and access patterns can be instrumental.

The WebAssembly memory model is designed to be compatible with JavaScript's garbage-collected heap. This design enables seamless interactions between the two. However, copying large chunks of data between JavaScript and WebAssembly memory can be expensive. Hence, for performance-critical tasks, it's advisable to perform operations directly in WebAssembly memory whenever possible.

There's ongoing work in the WebAssembly community to introduce garbage collection. This feature aims to simplify memory management, particularly when porting high-level languages to WebAssembly. However, with the benefits of automated memory management, developers might also need to be aware of potential garbage collection-induced pauses and their impact on performance.

Sample Program: Fine Tuning Memory

To demonstrate the practical aspect of fine-tuning memory in WebAssembly, you will take the profiling example from earlier in this chapter.

The WebAssembly module is profiling different algorithms to check their efficiency. One of these algorithms involves a large data set of integers to be sorted. Now we shall look to optimize memory usage for this sorting algorithm.

Use Data Segments Efficiently

Initially, the data segment might look something like:

```
(data (i32.const 0) "\00\01\02\03\04\05\06\07...")
```

You might choose to compress this data segment or only initialize necessary data segments, avoiding any redundant or unused data.

Memory Pooling

Instead of allocating memory every time we need it, allocate a large chunk in advance and reuse this memory.

In the source C++ code:

```
int* pool = new int[100000];  // Pool of 100,000 integers
```

Minimizing Global Variables

Review your C++ code and ensure that global variables are used sparingly. Only keep those that are absolutely necessary. And, if the algorithm uses linked lists and random access is frequent, consider switching to arrays.

Stack and Heap Management

Be cautious with dynamic memory allocations. For instance, the sorting algorithm before optimization is as below:

```
int* arr = new int[length];
// ... use arr ...
delete[] arr;
```

and now after optimization using memory pool:

```
int* arr = pool;  // Use previously allocated pool
// ... use arr ...
// No need to delete as you will reuse this memory
```

Compress Data Before Storage

If the algorithm deals with large data sets, consider compressing data before storing it in memory. This might involve integrating a compression library with your WebAssembly module.

If the WebAssembly module interacts with JavaScript often, especially with large data sets, try to minimize the data transfers. For instance, if you need to visualize the sorted data, instead of transferring the entire sorted array to JavaScript, consider sending only necessary statistics or a smaller sample.

Implementation with Emscripten

Compile the optimized C++ code using Emscripten, and specify initial and maximum memory if you have a clear idea of your memory requirements:

```
emcc -O3 sorting.cpp -s WASM=1 -s TOTAL_MEMORY=64MB -s ALLOW_MEMORY_GROWTH=0 -o sorting.js
```

Here, we specified a total memory of 64MB and disallowed memory growth to ensure efficient usage.

Once the optimized WebAssembly module is loaded in the browser, use browser developer tools to monitor memory usage. The optimized module should show reduced memory usage and possibly improved performance.

Remember, while these are some common techniques, the specifics would always depend on the nature and requirements of the individual application. Always profile and test rigorously to achieve the best results.

Leverage Chrome for Performance

Certainly, leveraging Chrome Developer Tools (DevTools) is an essential skill for developers wanting to diagnose and optimize WebAssembly performance.

To start, launch the Chrome browser and open your WebAssembly-hosting web page. Right-click anywhere on the page and select "Inspect", or alternatively use the shortcut Ctrl + Shift + I (or Cmd + Option + I on Mac). This opens the DevTools panel.

Sources Panel

Viewing WebAssembly Modules
Within the "Sources" panel, you'll find a left-hand sidebar that showcases the folder structure of your website or application. Here, any WebAssembly modules that have been loaded into the environment will be visible, identified by their .wasm file extensions. This provides an organized way to access and inspect the WebAssembly modules that are a part of your application.

Debugging Features
Chrome's developer tools offer the ability to set breakpoints directly in the WebAssembly code. Simply clicking on the line number where you wish to pause the execution sets a breakpoint. Once the program execution reaches this designated line, it will halt, allowing you to delve into variable states, examine the call stack, and investigate other relevant details of the program's state.

Memory Tab

Heap Snapshots
This useful feature grants you the ability to capture a full snapshot of the JavaScript heap at any given moment. By clicking on the "Take snapshot" button, you can then probe into objects, scrutinize their sizes, and view constructors. This is invaluable for detecting memory leaks within WebAssembly applications.

Allocation Profiles
The "Profiles" section enables you to record memory allocation over a certain time period. This is particularly insightful for WebAssembly applications, as you can monitor memory growth and pinpoint memory-intensive tasks or operations that may need optimization.

Performance Tab

Session Recording
At the top-left corner of the Performance tab, you'll find a record button. Clicking this and then interacting with your application—focusing particularly on the WebAssembly components—followed by stopping the recording, gives you an in-depth analysis of how the browser's time was utilized.

Performance Metrics Analysis
Once you've recorded a session, a timeline appears that details various performance metrics. You can zoom into specific segments to gain a deeper understanding of scripting durations, rendering intervals, and painting times, among other metrics.

Bottom-Up and Call Tree Analysis

These sub-sections in the Performance tab dissect the recorded session into individual function calls. It reveals which functions are consuming the most time and resources. You can specifically look for your WebAssembly functions or any JavaScript functions that engage with WebAssembly to identify potential performance bottlenecks.

Network Tab

WebAssembly Loading Metrics

As your application page loads, the Network tab captures all network requests, making them visible for inspection. By filtering these requests to focus on "Other," you can specifically look at WebAssembly files. This information can be crucial for understanding how long your WebAssembly module takes to load.

Size and Initialization Time Metrics

Here, you can review the file size of your .wasm modules. If you find that the file is excessively large, it may require optimization. Additionally, the tab shows how much time is needed to download and initialize the WebAssembly module, helping you identify potential areas for performance enhancement.

Console Tab

Interaction Logs

Should you use **console.log** statements within your JavaScript functions that communicate with WebAssembly, those logs will appear in this tab. This can offer valuable insights into the data being exchanged between JavaScript and WebAssembly, as well as flag any errors that might occur.

Application Tab

WebAssembly Data Storage

While WebAssembly itself doesn't come with direct storage capabilities, data stored through WebAssembly frameworks like Emscripten's FileSystem API can be examined in the Application tab. This tab lets you investigate any data stored in IndexedDB or Web Storage that may have been manipulated or accessed by WebAssembly modules.

Practical Steps with WebAssembly

1. Start by navigating to the webpage where your WebAssembly application is deployed. Open your browser's developer tools and go to the Performance tab. From here, initiate a recording session. During the recording, make sure to interact with specific portions of your web application that heavily rely on WebAssembly functionalities. This is essential because it will give you a clear performance overview of how well your WebAssembly code is functioning during real-time user interactions.

2. Once you've stopped the recording, your next step is to scrutinize the performance timeline. Look for any long frames, or 'janky' spots that could indicate performance bottlenecks or inefficiencies. Go into granular detail within these specific time frames to inspect the call stack. The goal here is to identify whether specific WebAssembly functions or modules are the root causes of any performance hiccups. Understanding the call stack will provide valuable insights into how each function interacts and may be affecting performance negatively.

3. After analyzing performance, switch over to the Memory tab in your browser's developer tools. Here, you'll want to take a snapshot of the current memory usage. Browse through this snapshot to check if there are unexpected objects or variables that are consuming large amounts of memory. Frequently, these could be large data arrays, buffers, or other types of variables used in your WebAssembly operations. Identifying and optimizing these can lead to noticeable performance improvements.

4. Move on to the Network tab to check on the load time of your WebAssembly (.wasm) file. If you notice that the file takes too long to load, it could be an indication that the file size is too large. In such cases, consider splitting your WebAssembly file into smaller chunks. Alternatively, you can also look into optimizing the .wasm file using specialized tools like Binaryen. This can help to reduce the file size, thereby speeding up load times and improving overall application performance.

5. Lastly, navigate to the Console tab within the developer tools. This space is crucial for diagnosing any runtime errors or warnings either from the WebAssembly code or the JavaScript code that interacts with it. The console output can give you direct insights into failed operations, data mismatches, or any other inconsistencies. Being familiar with the console will enable you to debug more efficiently, making it easier to identify the underlying issues affecting your WebAssembly application.

By utilizing Chrome DevTools, developers get a comprehensive toolkit to diagnose, debug, and optimize WebAssembly's performance. The key is iterative testing: make a change, test, and then analyze. Over time, these iterative improvements will significantly boost the performance and reliability of your WebAssembly applications. Remember, while DevTools provides vast amounts of data, the art lies in interpreting this data effectively to drive meaningful performance enhancements.

Perform Multithreading and Parallelism

Multithreading and parallelism are essential concepts for improving the performance of compute-intensive applications. WebAssembly (Wasm) is no different, and taking advantage of these principles can significantly boost your Wasm application's efficiency. We shall dive into implementing multithreading in WebAssembly.

WebAssembly Threads and Web Workers

WebAssembly threads are built on top of Web Workers. Web Workers allow you to run JavaScript and WebAssembly modules in the background, separate from the main thread, ensuring smooth UI performance. The SharedArrayBuffer is a type of buffer that can be used to share memory between the main thread and Web Workers, facilitating communication.

Ensure you're using a browser that supports multithreading in WebAssembly (most modern browsers do). And, your WebAssembly compiler i.e. Emscripten should have support for generating threaded code.

Consider our previous matrix multiplication example. For large matrices, computation can be intensive. We can parallelize this operation, allowing different threads to compute parts of the result.

Compiling with Emscripten

When compiling your C/C++ code to WebAssembly, ensure you enable threading:

```
emcc matrix_multiplication.cpp -o matrix.js -s USE_PTHREADS=1 -s PTHREAD_POOL_SIZE=n
```

Here, PTHREAD_POOL_SIZE=n preallocates n number of Web Workers for your application.

Updating Code

In our matrix multiplication, the nested loop can be parallelized. Using OpenMP (a parallel programming API), you can specify which parts of the code should run in parallel:

```
#pragma omp parallel for
for (int i = 0; i < N; i++) {
  for (int j = 0; j < N; j++) {
    for (int k = 0; k < N; k++) {
      result[i][j] += matrixA[i][k] * matrixB[k][j];
```

```
        }
    }
}
```

The #pragma omp parallel for directive will distribute iterations of the i loop among multiple threads.

HTML and JS Setup

Ensure that your web page's header has the Content Security Policy set up to allow for shared memory and data:

```
<meta http-equiv="Content-Security-Policy" content="script-src 'none';">
```

In your JavaScript (generated by Emscripten), initialize the Wasm module and provide functions to facilitate the data transfer between your main thread and Web Workers:

```
const matrixModule = {
    onRuntimeInitialized: function() {
        // Initialize or call functions after Wasm is ready.
    },
    mainScriptUrlOrBlob: "path_to_main_script.js", // path to the main JS file
};
```

Invoking the Parallel Code

From your JavaScript, you can now call the matrix multiplication function. The WebAssembly code will handle distributing the work among the Web Workers:

```
let matrixA = ... // Define matrix A
let matrixB = ... // Define matrix B
let result = matrixModule._multiplyMatrices(matrixA, matrixB); // Calling Wasm function
```

As with all optimizations, testing and measuring performance improvements in real-world scenarios are crucial to ensure the changes you make benefit the end-user.

Lazy Loading and Code Splitting

Lazy loading and code splitting are optimization techniques used to enhance the load performance and responsiveness of web applications. By leveraging these techniques, you can ensure that only the necessary code and resources are loaded on-demand, resulting in a faster initial load time and a more fluid user experience.

We shall see how to incorporate these practices into our previous examples.

Code Splitting: What Is It?

Code splitting is a development methodology that involves the separation of your codebase into multiple, distinct bundles or chunks. This is in contrast to the traditional approach where all code gets bundled into a single, monolithic file. The key advantage of code splitting is the ability to load only the portions of code that are immediately necessary for a given situation, thereby improving performance and reducing load times. When it comes to WebAssembly, the practice of code splitting gains even more significance. This is because WebAssembly modules are usually compiled from languages like C, C++, or Rust, resulting in larger file sizes compared to typical JavaScript files. By strategically splitting these larger compiled modules, you're able to serve only the parts needed for specific application functionalities, ensuring quicker load times and more efficient resource usage.

Lazy Loading: The Basics

Lazy loading is a technique aimed at optimizing the performance of web applications by deferring the initialization and execution of certain resources until they are explicitly required. Instead of burdening the browser with loading all modules or resources as soon as a web page is accessed, lazy loading allows you to only serve what is essential for the initial view. Additional modules or resources are loaded on-demand, typically in response to specific user interactions or actions, like clicking a button or scrolling down a page. This minimizes the amount of data that needs to be transferred and parsed at the start, resulting in faster initial load times. Moreover, in the context of WebAssembly, lazy loading can be exceedingly beneficial. Given that WebAssembly modules are often larger than conventional JavaScript files, deferring the loading of non-essential modules can yield substantial performance gains, allowing users to interact with key features of your application more swiftly.

Implementing Code Splitting

Identify Split Points

For our previous matrix multiplication example, assume that we have different matrix operations like addition, subtraction, and multiplication. Each operation can be a potential split point.

Compile Modules Separately

Compile each operation into a separate WebAssembly module:

```
emcc matrix_multiplication.cpp -o multiply.wasm
emcc matrix_addition.cpp -o add.wasm
```

This will create separate .wasm files for each operation.

Load Modules Dynamically

In your JavaScript, use dynamic imports to load the necessary WebAssembly module:

```
function performOperation(operationType, matrixA, matrixB) {
  switch(operationType) {
    case "multiply":
      import('./multiply.wasm').then(module => {
        // Call the function from the module
        module._multiplyMatrices(matrixA, matrixB);
      });
      break;
    // ... Handle other operations similarly
  }
}
```

Implementing Lazy Loading with WebAssembly

Determine Dependencies

Before you can lazily load a module, understand the dependencies. If moduleB depends on moduleA, ensure moduleA is loaded first.

Load Modules Dynamically

You can use the WebAssembly JavaScript API to dynamically load and instantiate Wasm modules:

```
let cachedModule;

function lazyLoadMatrixModule() {
  if (cachedModule) return Promise.resolve(cachedModule);
```

```
  return fetch('path_to_multiply.wasm')
    .then(response => response.arrayBuffer())
    .then(bytes => WebAssembly.instantiate(bytes))
    .then(results => {
      cachedModule = results.instance;
      return results.instance;
    });
}

function multiplyMatrices(matrixA, matrixB) {
  lazyLoadMatrixModule().then(module => {
    module.exports.multiplyMatrices(matrixA, matrixB);
  });
}
```

Here, the multiplyMatrices function will load the multiplication module only when called. Subsequent calls will use the cached module.

Integrate with User Interactions

For a more refined user experience, tie the lazy loading mechanism with user actions. For instance, only load the multiplication module when a user clicks a "Multiply Matrices" button.

Caching Strategies

Caching stands as a cornerstone optimization strategy, pivotal for enhancing the performance metrics of web applications. This tenet is universally true, and particularly applicable in the context of WebAssembly (Wasm) modules. Effective caching strategies can significantly mitigate the need for users to repeatedly download identical WebAssembly modules. The end result is markedly faster load times and a substantially smoother user interaction experience with your web application.

Why Cache WebAssembly Modules?

WebAssembly modules, especially those that are a part of complex, feature-rich applications, tend to be large in terms of file size. When these large files have to be downloaded every time a user opens your application, the consequences can be detrimental. The user experience can be marred significantly, more so if the user is operating on a sluggish network connection. By employing thoughtful caching strategies, you can substantially reduce load times, thereby mitigating issues that stem from repeated downloads and enhancing overall user satisfaction.

Browser's Native Cache Mechanism

Modern web browsers come equipped with built-in mechanisms designed specifically for caching various types of web assets. These include but are not limited to images, stylesheets, JavaScript files, and, relevant to our learnings, WebAssembly modules. During a user's inaugural visit to a website, these assorted assets are downloaded to the client machine and stored locally within the browser's native cache. For all subsequent visits to the same website, these browsers are engineered to load the assets directly from the cache. This mechanism bypasses the need for additional network fetches, serving to significantly expedite load times.

For WebAssembly Modules

When a user navigates to your application, modern browsers will automatically cache any WebAssembly modules identified by their .wasm file extensions. Upon any future visits to the application, the browser performs a validity check on the cache. If deemed valid, the WebAssembly module is fetched directly from the local cache rather than being downloaded again from the network. This system serves to drastically reduce the time taken to load the application, thereby contributing to a more efficient and enjoyable user experience.

Service Workers for Cache Control

Service Workers allow developers to programmatically manage caches. They operate in the background, separate from the web page, and provide intercepting fetch requests, managing cache behavior, and more.

Setting Up a Service Worker for WebAssembly Caching follows below steps:

Registering Service Worker

In your main JavaScript file:

```
if ('serviceWorker' in navigator) {
  navigator.serviceWorker.register('/service-worker.js').then(reg => {
    console.log('Service Worker registered successfully.', reg);
  });
}
```

Defining Caching Logic in Service Worker

In service-worker.js:

```
const CACHE_NAME = 'wasm-cache-v1';
const WASM_ASSETS = ['path_to/module1.wasm', 'path_to/module2.wasm'];

self.addEventListener('install', event => {
  event.waitUntil(
    caches.open(CACHE_NAME)
      .then(cache => cache.addAll(WASM_ASSETS))
  );
});

self.addEventListener('fetch', event => {
  event.respondWith(
    caches.match(event.request)
      .then(response => {
        if (response) return response;
        return fetch(event.request)
          .then(netResponse => {
            return caches.open(CACHE_NAME)
              .then(cache => {
                cache.put(event.request, netResponse.clone());
                return netResponse;
              });
          });
      })
  );
});
```

This script sets up the Service Worker to cache specific WebAssembly assets during installation and to use the cache for serving these assets on fetch requests.

Application-Level Caching with IndexedDB

Another strategy for caching Wasm modules is by using the IndexedDB API. IndexedDB is a low-level API for storing significant amounts of structured data, including files and blobs.

For WebAssembly

Wasm modules can be compiled and stored in IndexedDB. On subsequent visits, the application checks IndexedDB for the compiled module before attempting to fetch and compile.

Example:

```
// Check if the module exists in IndexedDB
function getCachedWasmModule(dbName, key) {
  return new Promise((resolve, reject) => {
    const openRequest = indexedDB.open(dbName);
    openRequest.onerror = () => reject(openRequest.error);
    openRequest.onsuccess = () => {
      const db = openRequest.result;
      const transaction = db.transaction("wasm-modules", "readonly");
      transaction.objectStore("wasm-modules").get(key).onsuccess = event => {
        if (event.target.result) {
          resolve(event.target.result);
        } else {
          reject('Module not found in cache');
        }
      };
    };
  });
}

// Usage
getCachedWasmModule("wasm-cache", "module1").then(module => {
  // Use the cached module
}).catch(() => {
  // Fetch, compile, and cache the module
});
```

Best Practices for Caching WASM Modules

Implementing caching strategies for WebAssembly modules can greatly improve the performance and user experience of your web applications. Whether you're using the browser's built-in mechanisms, service workers, or application-level storage like IndexedDB, effectively managing cache ensures quick access to resources and reduces redundant network requests.

Following are some of the measures you may keep in your check:

- Regularly Update Cache: Ensure users always get the latest and most secure versions of your assets.
- Fallback to Network: If the cache fails or isn't available, always have logic in place to fetch the module from the network.
- Monitor Cache Size: Keep an eye on the overall cache size. Over-relying on cache might cause storage issues for users.

Summary

This chapter delved deep into strategies that can transform a Wasm-based application's efficiency. Starting with profiling and benchmarking, we learned the importance of understanding where the bottlenecks lie in our Wasm code. Tools such as Chrome DevTools provided insights into our application's performance, pinpointing areas where optimization was crucial. By regularly monitoring and profiling, developers can ensure that their Wasm applications remain performant, even as they evolve and scale.

Memory management in Wasm stands out as a paramount concern. WebAssembly's linear memory model offers both challenges and opportunities. By understanding the intricacies of memory allocation, deallocation, and garbage collection, developers can fine-tune memory utilization to enhance the performance and reduce wastage. Memory tuning doesn't just improve speed but also ensures that applications are efficient in resource-constrained environments.

With the foundational knowledge of performance in place, we ventured into the realm of browser tools. The Chrome Developer Tools (DevTools) emerged as a valuable ally for anyone keen to dive into the granular details of their Wasm application's performance in a real-world setting. From profiling CPU usage to monitoring network requests, DevTools provided a holistic view, guiding developers in making informed optimization decisions.

But performance optimization isn't solely about introspection. External strategies, such as multithreading and parallelism, offer avenues to distribute computational loads, making applications faster and more responsive. WebAssembly's support for threads via the threading proposal allows developers to harness the full power of modern multi-core processors, bringing desktop-level performance to web applications. Furthermore, lazy loading and code splitting presented techniques to load only the essential parts of an application initially, reducing the initial load time and enhancing the user experience. This approach ensures resources are fetched and utilized only when necessary, making applications nimble.

Finally, the chapter emphasized the importance of caching in WebAssembly. Caching strategies, ranging from leveraging browser's native mechanisms to sophisticated service workers and IndexedDB storage solutions, help in reducing redundant network requests and ensure rapid access to Wasm modules. Proper caching not only boosts performance but also offers a seamless user experience, especially in network-constrained scenarios.

Throughout this chapter, the recurring theme has been the continuous pursuit of excellence. Whether you're diagnosing issues, fine-tuning memory, or leveraging advanced browser tools and caching strategies, the goal remains clear: delivering the fastest, most efficient WebAssembly applications to users.

Thank You

Index

A

B

C

D

E

F

G

H

I

J

L

M

N

O

P

R

S

T

W

Epilogue

As we reach the final pages of our journey through the world of WebAssembly, it is clear just how transformative this technology is. When we began, WebAssembly was shrouded in mystery, its inner workings obscure. Now, having explored its core concepts and capabilities in depth, we can truly appreciate its elegance and potential. Through practical demonstrations and real-world examples, we have not just learned what WebAssembly is, but what it enables us to build. The ability to run near-native code on the web unlocks new dimensions of performance, efficiency and user experience. Yet, as we discovered, with great power comes great responsibility. To harness WebAssembly's full potential requires meticulous skill and strategic optimization.

Our expedition illuminated the tools that make WebAssembly so versatile. Emscripten, Binaryen, JavaScript interfaces and more - each technology we covered showcased new ways to leverage WebAssembly's speed while integrating seamlessly into existing development workflows. Far from replacing JavaScript, WebAssembly enhances it, enabling more responsive applications that users love. Beyond performance, our deeper revelations were about the essence of good software - the user's experience. We realized that all the technical intricacies explored here have one purpose - to create seamless, efficient applications. In an age of fleeting attention, ensuring accessibility and lightning-fast experiences is paramount. This will be WebAssembly's lasting impact.

Though this book concludes, your journey is just beginning. You now have an enriched palette - both conceptual knowledge and practical skills - to build your own vision. The world of web development will keep evolving, but you have all the tools to evolve with it. Stay curious, keep learning and create applications that make the web faster, more powerful and more delightful.

As you venture forth, remember - technology comes and goes, but great user experiences are timeless. Build with skill, optimize with care, and keep your user at the heart of all you create. Wherever your path leads next, may it be transformative. Godspeed, developer - the future is yours to shape.

www.ingramcontent.com/pod-product-compliance
Lightning Source LLC
Chambersburg PA
CBHW080215170726
48282CB00030B/1124
* 9 7 8 8 1 1 9 1 7 7 2 5 7 *